SURE THING COMMODITY TRADING

HOW SEASONAL FACTORS INFLUENCE COMMODITY PRICES

SURE THING COMMODITY TRADING

HOW SEASONAL FACTORS INFLUENCE COMMODITY PRICES

by
Larry R. Williams
and
Michelle L. Noseworthy

Windsor Books, Brightwaters, N.Y.

Published by Windsor Books
P.O. Box 280
Brightwaters, N.Y. 11718

ISBN 0-930233-04-2

To Fred:

My contribution to this book would have never been completed without your total support of my work. Thank you.

Love, Michelle

It is a good thing the Norsmen were not playing when we were around—no one would have ever discovered us with that kind of competition!

Phil and Don

CONTENTS

HOW TO USE THIS BOOK

There are five ways one can use the research presented in this book. The ways should ultimately end in better trading, or more profits, for the trader or investor.

The first way one can use the book is simply as we have presented it, taking all of the trades in a particular commodity or group of commodities by the rules as we have given them. We feel certain that these seasonal tendencies will be repeated in the future and that we will see a similar track record of profit and losses in the coming years.

Secondly, one can use the data contained here to identify long, long in advance——actually years in advance——probable trends that a particular market will have. As an example, we know there is a strong tendency for wheat prices to decline in the first part of the year. Knowing this, of course, we are going to be more on the lookout for sell signals during this time period and demand more from buy signals during what is a normal time for prices to decline.

Thirdly, a trader can use the data presented here to locate and spot seasonal trades of his own. As complete as we feel our research has been—and there have been hundreds of hours identifying and finding these tendencies—we're certain it is just like fishing; there's still some big ones out there which we did not capture. We're not certain how many more there are, and we think we've pinpointed the major ones; however, we will continue our work to find additional seasonal tendencies and hope others do, too. If we find additional seasonal tendencies which are of value, we will endeavor, to the best of our ability, to publish this new information in subsequent editions of this book.

Fourthly, one can use the trade ideas presented here to establish the validity of seasonal tendencies and use seasonal tendencies in conjunction with intermediate term cycles that are offered in the market. If you have isolated, say, a 32-week cycle in cattle and you know it calls for an approximate low the first part of the year, this would be extremely interesting, given the fact that cattle prices have rallied during the first of the year in most instances we have studied.

Finally, we suppose one will be able to get additional value from the book in that, up until this point, no one has known, on a factual basis, what the real seasonal tendencies and interaction of seasonal price patterns are in the market. The reader of this book now knows for sure, beyond a shadow of a doubt, what the seasonal tendencies and patterns of commodities have been.

A HANDY REFERENCE

Frequently, the trader or even broker, is inundated with advice on what is supposed to be a seasonal tendency. However, when we've checked out these "ideas", we have discovered that the majority of them have never been in existence in the market or, if they have, they have only been offered for two or three years. Frankly, two or three years' data is not assurance enough for us to enter a seasonal trade. Thus, you now have a great reference to check out stories about seasonal tendencies to see if they are real.

We believe that any trade that has shown an accuracy of 85% or more should definitely be considered on in the future. Those which have been 100% accurate, of course, are going to be the ones that everyone is going to follow, and we will probably trade ourselves. There are some trades that are real standouts, such as the egg trades; more than that, we just don't see how traders can fail to take advantage of these excellent opportunities in wheat, cattle and pork bellies.

However, most people will not take advantage of these seasonal tendencies. Despite the fact that someone has paid a large sum of money for this book, knows the data, knows how reliable the seasonal tendency is, we suspect that most people will be afraid to put on the seasonal trade.

DISCIPLINE IS NEEDED

That's right, afraid. Why? Simply because they don't know what is going to happen in the future. We've got news for you; we don't know either. However, we do believe that one of the better ways of judging what will happen in the future is an analysis of the past and, given that most trades have stop points or reversal points, we feel comfortable, as professional traders, in knowing that even if the seasonal tendency does not work we are well protected in the event market prices reverse in just about all the trades we have presented. It will take discipline to follow the trade rules we have outlined. However, it takes discipline to live correctly, and it also takes discipline to trade the markets correctly.

SOME PEOPLE WE WOULD LIKE TO THANK

In preparing this book, we have used several sources and received help from some personal friends whom we would like to acknowledge at this time.

To begin with, Edward Dobson's books, COMMODITY SPREADS: HISTORICAL CHART PERSPECTIVE, as well as COMMODITIES: A CHART ANTHOLOGY, have been invaluable. These works can be purchased from Mr. Dobson at Box 10344, Greenville, SC 29603. Mr. Dobson's spread book is a must for spread traders and his Chart Anthology presents daily high, low and close for most all actively followed commodities since 1961. This particular reference was invaluable in helping us isolate and locate probable time periods when seasonal tendencies are operative. Mr. Dobson has contributed a great deal to the market place and his work should be respected.

Some seasonal tendency work was done several years ago by Mr. Philip Berkley, Berkley Associates, 132 West Broadway, San Diego, California 92101. We have studied Mr. Berkley's work and some of our work is similar to his; however, there are many seasonal trades Mr. Berkley has suggested which we have avoided. There are also some where we have similarities in our work. This is not due to our plagiarizing his work, far from it. It is simply a fact that we both see the same thing in the markets, because that same thing is there.

Future Research, Box 6115, Alexandria, Virginia 22306, has also an interesting compilation of seasonal tendencies with trade rules. We do not have a copy of their work. However, we have seen some of their data and have found it most interesting.

Another book which has been very helpful to us in understanding the markets is COMMODITY FUTURES GAME by Teweles, Harlow & Stone. And, of course, we want to mention one of the author's books, Larry Williams, HOW I MADE ONE MILLION DOLLARS LAST YEAR TRADING COMMODITIES, $25, 850 Munras #2, Monterey, CA 93940.

We also want to acknowledge that our data has come from two sources. MJK Associates, 2600 Augustin Dr., Santa Clara, CA, is owned by Michael Marriott. MJK maintains one of the most extensive and clean computerized listings of commodity prices in the world. They are as reliable and accurate as you'll find. Our other source, Merlin System, 1044 Northern Blvd., Roslyn, NY 11576 has supplied the bulk of our data and we have found them to be an excellent source for data.

Finally, we want to thank some personal friends who have helped us gather needed data, notably Lee Turnbull, a broker with Paine, Webber, Jackson & Curtis, in Seattle, Washington and Al Alessandra, a broker with Shearson Hayden Stone in Palos Verdes, CA. Additionally, we would like to personally thank Stacy Tinkham for clerical work she provided in getting back prices and Thelma Lambert for her constant support and work in getting this book ready.

We hope that commodity traders and students throughout the world will appreciate our work and enjoy it as much as we have enjoyed compiling the data. Frankly, we often times feel we are more interested in obtaining and discovering market insight and knowledge than we are in the pure profits that come from the market. But, that's what probably makes us so research oriented.

We love to delve into unmapped areas and map them. This has been an attempt to map what has been a very much uncharted area of commodity price activity. Hopefully, other mapping attempts will be made in the future by ourselves and others that will provide even additional insight into seasonal tendencies of the commodity markets. However, for now, we feel we have presented an extremely good compilation of seasonal tendencies and seasonal trades with absolute mechanical rules that should continue to be profitable in the future.

We hope you are able to profit from the seasonal tendencies either by following the trades themselves or by using these tendencies to further improve your understanding of market operations.

PUBLISHER'S NOTE: All books referenced in this book, as well as many other fine books on the Commodities market, are available from Windsor Books, Box 280, Brightwaters, NY 11718. Write for a free comprehensive and descriptive catalog.

WHAT THE SEASONAL TENDENCIES LOOK LIKE

The purpose of this chapter is to show you a graphic presentation of the usual seasonal tendency for the majority of commodities. We are doing this with the aid of seasonal tendency charts published by Clayton Brokerage Firm, 7701 Forsythe Blvd., St. Louis, Missouri 63105.

In Larry Williams' first commodity book, HOW I MADE ONE MILLION DOLLARS LAST YEAR TRADING COMMODITIES, perhaps the first comprehensive collection of charts of seasonal tendencies was shown. Since that publication, we have additional seasonal data for the market and we feel the Clayton charts are a good representation of the seasonal tendencies. We will show all charts and give some brief comments on the various commodities.

The following charts are reprinted from Larry Williams' book and the second set of charts are reprinted from charts prepared by Clayton Brokerage Company headquartered in St. Louis, Missouri.

SEASONAL TENDENCY CHART

18

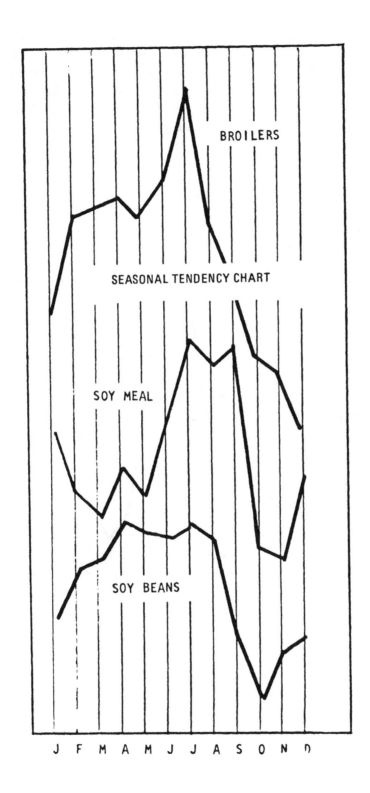

BROILERS

SEASONAL TENDENCY CHART

SOY MEAL

SOY BEANS

J F M A M J J A S O N D

19

BELLIES

Bellies and hogs trade with a similar seasonal tendency as you can see from the pork belly seasonal chart. Again, as with the entire meat complex, we tend to see pork belly highs occurring in August and lows occurring in the March-April time period. Also, notice the month of November represents a nice buying spot. We have a good seasonal trade to take advantage of that action.

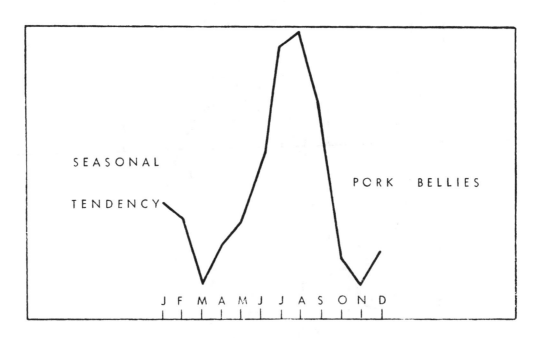

COCOA

Cocoa, as the charts show, has a proven seasonal tendency to rally from the February lows into the October highs. From the October highs we can expect the price to decline into and through the winter months. The price of cocoa starts the year on the down side for the first two quarters of the year. If upside activity is to be expected on a seasonal basis, it will most likely enter the market in July and August.

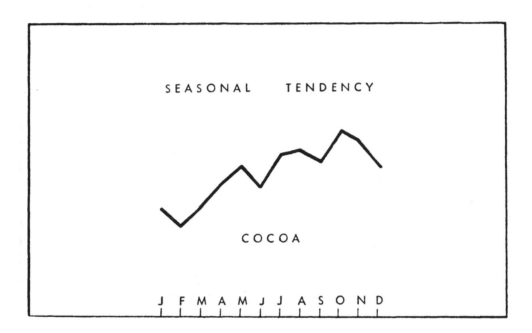

COPPER

Copper has a marked tendency to advance from January lows into August highs and we have developed several seasonal trades based on this overall tendency. Incidentally, this is one of the strongest seasonal tendencies in the market.

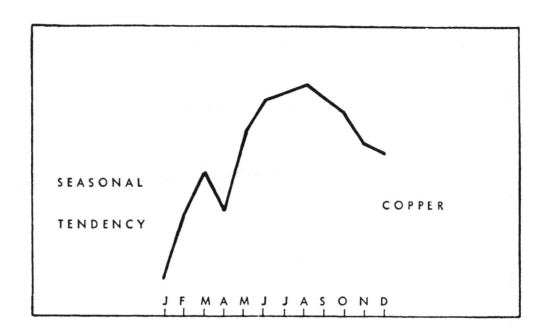

SEASONAL

TENDENCY

COPPER

J F M A M J J A S O N D

CORN

The price of corn usually sees a rally beginning in the spring of the year which reaches its zenith in the July - August time frame. This is typical of what happens with the meat prices, since livestock animals rely a great deal on corn for feed.

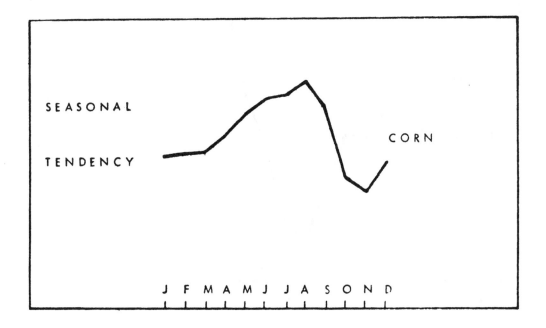

EGGS

Egg prices, as you will know from studying this book, have an extremely strong tendency to rally during April, May and June. It shows in the seasonal tendency chart, as you can see.

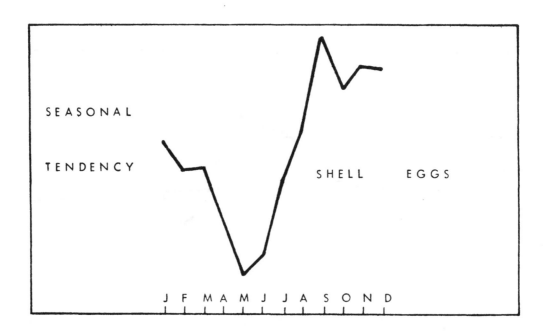

SEASONAL

TENDENCY   SHELL   EGGS

J F M A M J J A S O N D

GOLD

We are showing the seasonal tendency chart on gold for historical reference. We do not have enough data on the way gold trades to establish any strong seasonal tendencies at this time.

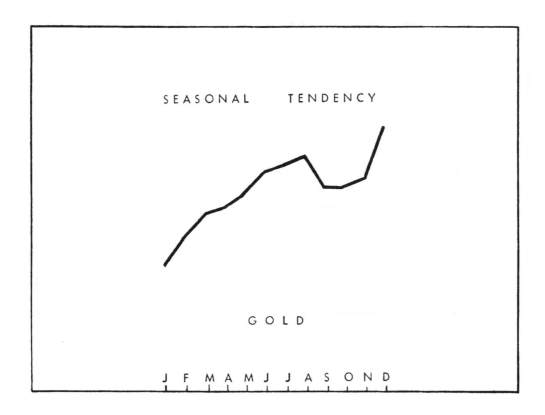

HOGS

Here you can expect a seasonal peak in the July - August time frame, with a summer rally starting sometime in May or June.

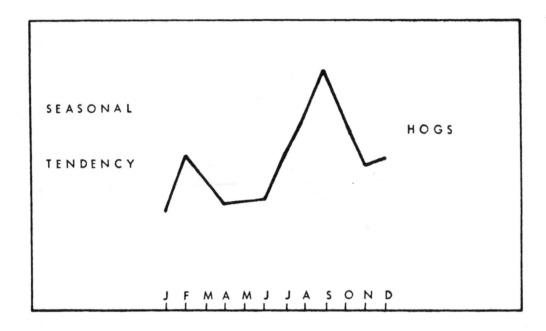

SEASONAL

TENDENCY

HOGS

J F M A M J J A S O N D

ICED BROILERS

We have isolated a few trades for iced broilers. However, you will notice that there is not much price-swing action in terms of the seasonal tendency for broilers. It should be noted that they usually see a high in the July - August period with the rest of the meat complex.

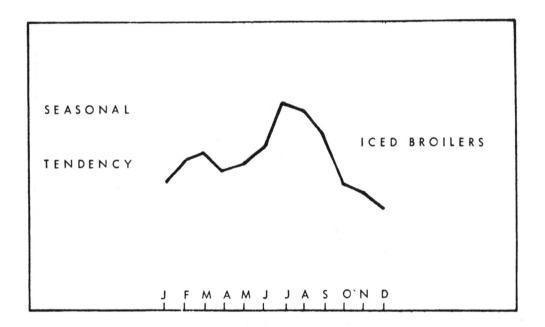

SEASONAL

TENDENCY

ICED BROILERS

J F M A M J J A S O N D

LIVE CATTLE

The seasonal tendency for cattle prices has been to rally during the spring of the year, reaching a high during the July - August time frame. In talking with cattle producers, farmers and ranchers, it's interesting to note how many of them are not aware of this strong tendency for cattle prices to advance during the first part of the year.

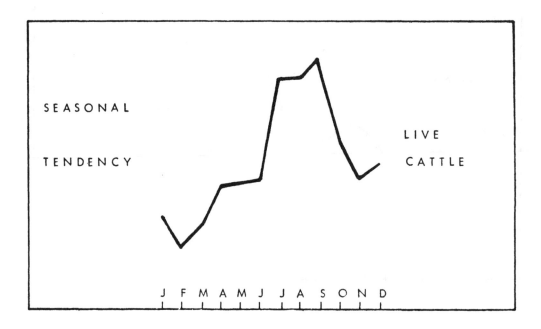

SEASONAL

TENDENCY

LIVE

CATTLE

J F M A M J J A S O N D

OATS

Oats are one of the best seasonal tendency traders, as you will notice from reading our trading rules. The tendency is for oat prices to decline into July and then start their bull move during the July lows and continue into December.

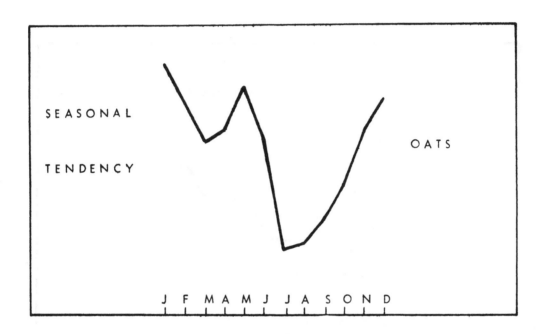

29

ORANGE JUICE

Frankly, we have had difficulty finding extremely good trades for orange juice. This is well illustrated in the orange juice chart which shows the strong seasonal move down from the January to July time period. The one orange juice trade we did discover capitalizes on this downtrend move. The uptrend that the orange juice shows, starting in July through December, may or may not occur, depending on crop factors, etc.

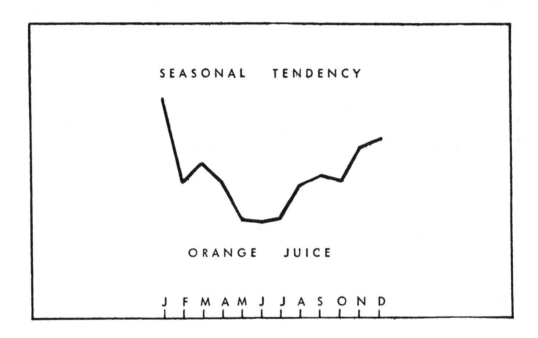

SEASONAL TENDENCY

ORANGE JUICE

J F M A M J J A S O N D

PLYWOOD AND LUMBER

One of the strongest seasonal tendencies is for the price of plywood and lumber to rally during the first part of the year. We have developed several trades that take advantage of this rally. However, we have had difficulty in constructing a profitable seasonal trade that takes advantage of the decline from the March highs to the November lows. This period doesn't seem to have such a strong seasonal tendency.

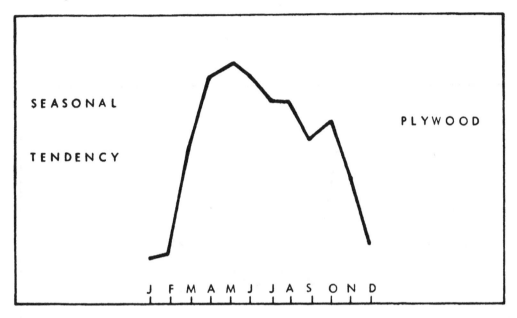

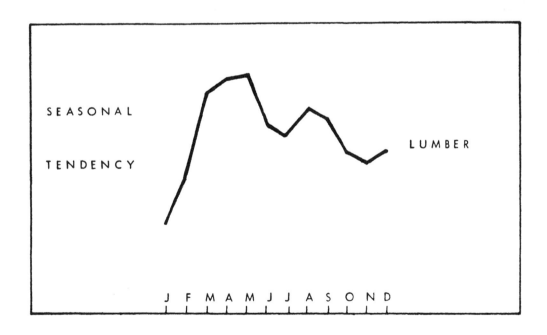

SILVER

Although we have not covered silver on a seasonal tendency basis, we are showing a seasonal tendency chart for silver. Prior to the gargantuan bull market move in 1974 silver did not have a well-defined seasonal tendency and we feel silver, like sugar, is one of the more difficult commodities in which to isolate seasonal trades.

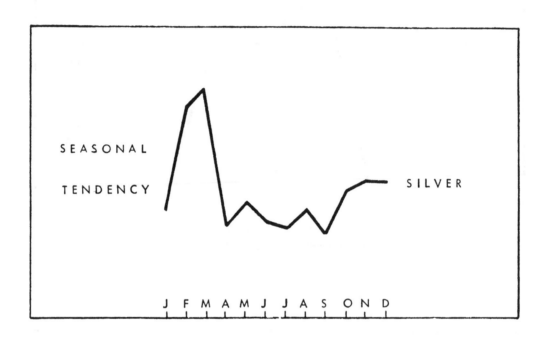

SOYBEANS

Soybeans tend to rally into the summer months and then decline as the crop is being harvested during August, September and October. One of the strongest tendencies is for soybeans to rally in January. Soybean meal does not follow soybeans.

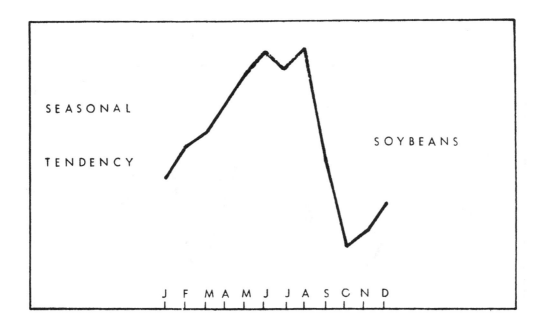

SOYBEAN MEAL

Despite what many analysts say, the seasonal tendency charts make it very clear that soybean meal does not follow the price of soybeans. You can see from a quick glance at the charts that soybean meal has rallies and declines with a greater magnitude and, to some extent, different time periods than the soybeans themselves. The seasonal tendency you want to look for is a rally starting in the March-April time period, peaking out in the July-August time period.

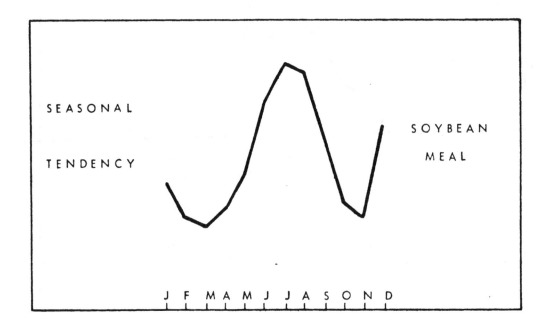

SEASONAL

TENDENCY

SOYBEAN

MEAL

J F M A M J J A S O N D

SOYBEAN OIL

Soybean oil has some erratic seasonal tendencies. Despite the charts shown, the tendency is not quite as clear as it appears here, because in our own personal study it has covered more years than the Clayton people used for their soybean oil seasonal tendency chart. We find that soybean oil tends to have a low in the July - August time period; however, it does not peak out until some time into November or December.

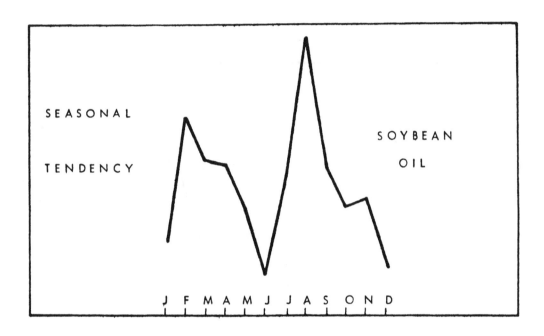

SUGAR

Sugar, which we have not covered in this book, has a tendency to decline during the first part of the year. According to this chart, sugar then bottoms during the middle of the year and rallies towards the end of the year in December. However, we believe this seasonal tendency chart is influenced a great deal by the 1974 sugar bull market. Our own study shows that the normal tendency for sugar is for a rally to start during the April-May time period and last into July. It then seems to decline from July to October. What this all adds up to is that the seasonal tendencies in sugar are not well defined.

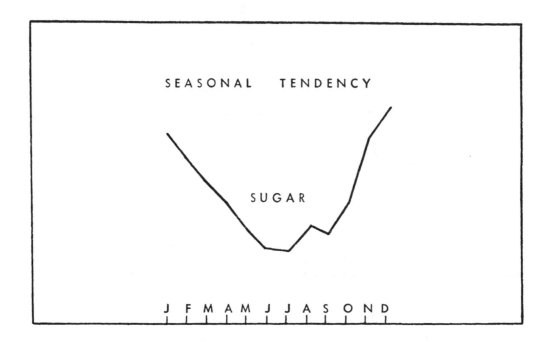

THREE MONTH TREASURY BILL YIELDS

We do not have enough data to construct trade rules for treasury bills at this date, but we thought you would enjoy a chart of what usually happens with interest rates.

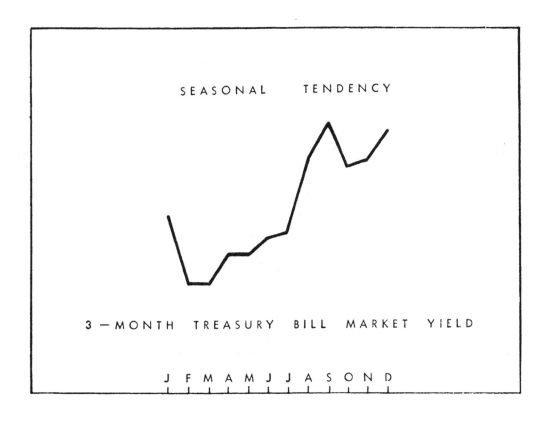

SEASONAL   TENDENCY

3 — MONTH   TREASURY   BILL   MARKET   YIELD

J F M A M J J A S O N D

WHEAT

The seasonal tendency chart on wheat makes it appear that wheat bottoms with a high degree of regularity in the July - August period; however, in trying to put together a seasonal tendency trade, we have had difficulties in establishing how one should enter the market for this tendency.

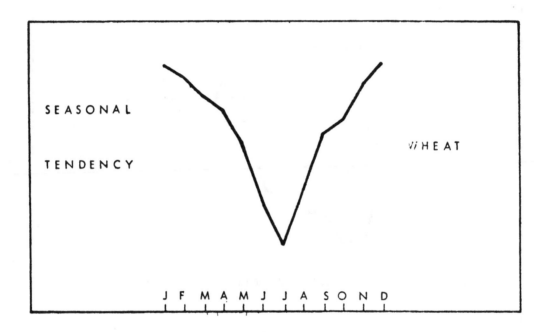

CATTLE

The ultimate price for cattle is a reflection of several factors in the marketplace. Unlike other commodities, there are more hands involved in the processing of cattle. To begin with, ranchers have to buy breeding stock or raise their own. To feed the animals, they have to buy grain from grain farmers, so grain farmers also enter into the picture. Next, of course, there are feeders — that is, large feeding lot operations where cattle are fed and fattened for final marketing. The next step in the line, of course, becomes the slaughter houses where the animals are killed and broken down into various parts which are then sold through retailers, such as Safeway, A & P, etc., before ultimately ending up in the hands of the consumer. As you can see, there are many steps and, of course, each step inflates the price of cattle from the previous purchase price if everyone in the chain is to make profits.

There are some important reports for the cattle market. Perhaps the most important one would be the monthly Cold Storage report, as well as the Cattle and Calves reports. The monthly Cold Storage report has been interesting in recent trading years in that whatever the market has done the day following the monthly Cold Storage report has been the incorrect thing to do. In other words, if the market was down the day following a monthly Cold Storage report, recently, it's been almost a sure-thing trade that the market will reverse and go in an up direction following that report.

According to most authorities it takes approximately three years from the time that a cow is bred until the consumer barecues his dinner. However, this cycle does not seem to be apparent in cattle prices themselves, and it may be accelerated due to new breeding techniques, etc. The main emphasis on the animals, after they're born of course, is to get them fat and as large as possible in as short a time span as possible. The average animal will be slaughtered when he is somewhere between twenty-four and thirty months old and will weigh between 1,000 and 1,200 pounds. Slaughtering of the animals remains pretty stable throughout the year; however, it tends to be higher in the fall, especially October and November, and a little bit lower in the spring or in the early mid-winter, such as a February-March time period. Because of this, we have usually seen some pressure in the market; however, these presures, that one would expect from the end of the production cycle (the slaughter of cattle), do not seem to be apparent in the seasonal tendency trades that we have established in the market.

It is interesting to note that cattle represent the largest agricultural crop that this country produces; in fact, most estimates are that the United States raises approximately ten percent of all the cattle in the world. The value of the cattle crop is similiar to the total combined value of wheat, corn, soybeans and cotton.

Those who follow the beef market, as well as the grain market, must realize that the largest use of grains in this country is not for human consumption but for animal consumption and, of the animal consumption, cattle consume more grains than anything else.

A one-cent move in cattle is worth $400. There are various months to trade. The most popular months are perhaps the April, August and December contracts. Overall, the price trend for cattle is tending to be on an upward basis. This is due largely to inflation, the inflated prices of agriculture products due to a shrinkage of land, and the increase of grain cost. The big factor, of course, for cattle traders to watch for will be grain costs.

CATTLE TRADE #1

The first cattle trade we were able to isolate starts the very first trading day of the year.

Since 1965, the seasonal tendency trade here has been 75% correct. In other words, it has been wrong three times out of the last 12 years. An analysis of the trade shows that the greatest loss incurred in any one year was 100 points or $400, with the largest gain in any year being 300 points or $1,200. This, of course, fits well within a risk/reward ratio of three to one.

The total gain over the twelve-year time period has been $7,228.

Trade Rules:

The trade is simple. On the first trading day in January you purchase long one contract of April cattle at the closing price of that day. You then place a stop one hundred points below the price where you entered the market. Place an order to take profits at 300 points above the price where you purchased. Finally, if you have not been stopped out or taken a profit by the first day in April, one should liquidate April 1.

Let's follow some examples of the trade to see how the trade worked out. In 1965 one purchased at 23.45, which meant you would have a straight stop at 22.45. Fortunately, that stop was not hit. By the same token one would place a target to take profits 300 points above the price of 23.45 or 26.45.

Unfortunately, prices did not rally to 26.45, so we would liquidate the trade on April 1. That was done at a price of 24.95, netting 150 points profit for the year of 1965.

CATTLE TRADE #1

	Price on 1st Trading Day of Year	USE OF 100-POINT STOP		LIQUIDATE AT TARGET		Liquidate on April 1	Profit/ Loss
		Stopped Out Date	Price	Date	Price		
1965	23.45					24.95	+150
1966	27.40					28.15	+75
1967	27.27	Jan 19	26.27				-100
1968	24.95					27.07	+212
1969	27.00			Mar 10	30.00		+300
1970	30.05			Mar 11	33.05		+300
1971	29.42			Feb 1	32.42		+300
1972	32.80					34.50	+170
1973	41.47			Feb 23	44.47		+300
1974	51.72			Jan 10	54.70		+300
1975	40.42	Jan 2	39.42				-100
1976	40.67	Jan 8	39.67				-100

75% CORRECT IN 12 YEARS
2107 POINTS PROFIT
300 POINTS LOSS
$7,228 NET PROFIT

Rules:
1. Buy long one contract of April Cattle on the first trading day of the year on the close.
2. Use a 100-point stop.
3. Take profits at 300 points above the purchase price.
4. If you have not been stopped out or taken a profit by April 1, liquidate position.

41

Considering the risk/reward factors of this trade, we feel it is one of the better seasonal tendency trades. Of course, most all of the seasonal tendency trades are exceptionally good. That is because we have carefully weeded out marginal trades, or trades that may be due to statistical coincidence more than seasonal factors.

There are many other trades that we could have presented in this publication; however, we did not feel that they were as reliable as the ones presented here or offered potential investors the correct risk/reward ratios.

CATTLE TRADE #2

There has been a strong seasonal tendency for the price of cattle to rally in the spring of the year. However, it is difficult to pinpoint the exact time when this rally will begin. The other seasonal tendency work we have seen that has tried to establish spring rallies, has been subject to several severe whipsaws.

The rules have produced six trades since 1965 and all have been profitable. So, of course, it rates high with a 100% batting average. The net profit is also good in that it produced 19.07 cents or $7,628.

After studying the results, it became obvious what the problems were, and what, indeed, would signal that we were going to have a spring rally. Essentially what we discoverd was, if prices for August cattle were higher on April 1 that they were on February 1, one could then, at that time, expect a rally in cattle prices. However, if prices were the same or lower than they were on the first day of February, one should not enter the market.

Trade Rules:

The trade rules are simple. Check the prices of August cattle on February 1 and then note if they are higher on April 1. If prices are higher on April 1, buy long. The next rule is to take profits on the 15th day of June. If one had followed these rules since 1965, the trade would have shown a profit in every year.

CATTLE TRADE #2

	Feb 1	Apr 1		June 15	Profit/ Loss
1965	23.85	24.70		26.77	+207
1966	28.45	27.55	NO TRADE		
1967	27.15	26.42	NO TRADE		
1968	25.75	26.10		26.95	+85
1969	27.15	29.35		32.10	+275
1970	31.45	30.92	NO TRADE		
1971	31.73	31.25	NO TRADE		
1972	32.97	33.15		36.62	+347
1973	43.77	43.50	NO TRADE		
1974	53.22	47.97	NO TRADE		
1975	37.20	40.37		49.30	+893
1976	43.55	44.75		45.75	+100

100% CORRECT IN 6 YEARS
1907 POINTS PROFIT
$7,628 NET PROFIT

Rules:
1. Check prices of August cattle on February 1 and then note if they are higher on April 1.
2. If prices are higher on April 1, buy long.
3. Take profits on June 15.

CATTLE TRADE #3

The next seasonal trade also attempts to capitalize on these tendencies for prices to rally in the spring, but this one is done on a little different basis. Both trades try to work the spring rally attempt but this trade does not have as high a batting average. Nonetheless, it is impressive because its gross dollar profits are larger.

The trade has been correct 75% of the time netting some $10,544 in profits. That is quite a bit considering the cattle market is not one of the most volatile commodities.

Trade Rules:

Buy long August cattle the first Friday in March. Use a stop that is the low of the year. In other words when you buy in March, check to see what the lowest low has been since January 1 and use that low as the stop. If you buy at the low of the year, the stop is the low of the week you buy or the next week's low, whichever is lower. Liquidate the position on June 1.

The greatest loss that occurred was in 1974 when there was a loss of 2.92 cents on the trade. It should be noted that the 1973-1975 time period was the most volatile in the history of cattle. The simplicity of this trade is nice to follow and we certainly feel that traders and investors should follow this trade in the future.

CATTLE TRADE #3

| | Buy Long | | Stop | | Liquidate June 1 | Profit/ Loss |
	Price	Date	Price	Date		
1965	24.02	Mar 5			27.65	+363
1966	28.75	Mar 4	28.15	Mar 14		-60
1967	26.45	Mar 1			27.62	+117
1968	26.12	Mar 1			26.32	+20
1969	28.92	Mar 7			32.80	+388
1970	31.85	Mar 6	30.35	Apr 14		-150
1971	30.32	Mar 5			31.57	+125
1972	32.83	Mar 3			35.95	+312
1973	44.15	Mar 2			47.40	+325
1974	49.27	Mar 1	46.35	Mar 26		-292
1975	35.77	Mar 7			46.75	+1098
1976	43.50	Mar 5			47.40	+390

75% CORRECT IN 12 YEARS
3138 POINTS PROFIT
502 POINTS LOSS
$10,544 NET PROFIT

Rules:
1. Buy long August cattle the first Friday in March.
2. Use a stop that is the low of the year since January 1.
3. If you buy at the low of the year, the stop is then the low of the week you bought long or the next week's low, whichever is lower.
4. Liquidate the position on June 1.

CATTLE TRADE #4

This next trade is one of the most exciting and interesting seasonal tendencies in the entire market place. If you go back and carefully study cattle price action, you will notice that the last three or four years have seen substantial declines beginning in August of each year. However, if you try to construct a seasonal tendency trade on that data, you will find that you are going to have a great many losses from 1964 up to 1972.

The interesting point we noticed after trying many different ways to handle this trade was that what seems to happen in the month of August is that cattle are very prone at this time to establish a new trend in the market. This may be the reversal of an existing trend, but in any event, a new and substantial trend is established. Therefore, once we had this realization, we began working with some trade rules and came up with the most profitable trade in cattle.

Since 1965 this trade has been 92% correct, which means it has been wrong only one time since 1965 and that occurred in 1970. The trade has produced 59.41 cents profit and has lost 6.90 cents with a net profit of 52.51 cents producing a total dollar gain of $21,004. That is substantial and marks this as the most dollar profitable trade we have encountered in the cattle seasonal tendency study.

Trade Rules:

The trade rules are simple. Buy long one contract of April cattle on August 15. Place a stop which is equal to 2.5% of the value on the closing price of August 15, and reverse if that stop is touched so we will be net short two contracts. If stopped out after December 1, do not reverse; just accept the loss. Liquidate the position, whether you are long or short, on December 15.

Let's take a year to run through as an example how the trade would work and would not work. In the year 1975, April cattle sold at 43.05 on the 15th trading day in August. The stop would be .025 percent multiplied by 43.05 which is 1.07. If we subtract 1.07 from 43.05, we have a stop of 41.98. Now it just so happened that on October 7, the stop was hit so we would sell three contracts and be short net two contracts at 41.98. We have a loss of 107 points from the long position and are short on October 7 two contracts. We would liquidate these two contracts on December 15 at 40.85 taking profits of 113 cents on each contract or a total profit of 226 cents for the year, minus a loss of 107 points, leaving us on the profitable side of the trade.

One of the interesting aspects of this trade is that regardless of what the market is going to do during the months of August through December, the trade is going to have you in the market and most likely in a profitable trade.

The one drawback to this trade is what happens if you buy long, sell short and then the market begins a substantial upmove. In the past this event has never occurred. However, in the event this occurs, you would want to use a stop that would probably be equal to the high seen in August. At that point, one would have the option of reversing his position to the long side or simply exiting the market. Since this would be such an unusual event, we would want to reverse and that would be the safeguard for this trade. If prices do get above the August high, reverse to the long side.

CATTLE TRADE #4

| | Buy Long Aug. 15 | REVERSAL TO SELL SHORT | | | STOPPED OUT WITH NO REVERSAL | | Liquidate | Profit/ Loss |
		2.5% Stop	Date	Loss	Price	Date	December 15	
1965	24.90	24.28					27.27	+237
1966	28.87	28.15	Sept 8	-.72			27.00	+230
1967	27.17	26.50	Sept 11	-.67			25.02	+296
1968	25.42	24.79					27.07	+165
1969	27.65	26.96					30.82	+317
1969	27.65	26.96					30.82	+317
1970	28.70	27.99			27.99	Dec 2		- 71
1971	31.07	30.30					32.37	+130
1972	34.55	33.69					40.40	+585
1973	59.07	57.60	Aug 17	-1.47			47.37	+2046
1974	45.97	44.83	Aug 19	-1.14			42.55	+456
1975	43.05	41.98	Oct 7	-1.07			40.85	+226
1976	44.95	43.83	Aug 30	-1.12			39.15	+936

92% CORRECT IN 13 YEARS
5,941 POINTS PROFIT
690 POINTS LOSS
21,004 NET PROFIT

Rules:
1. Buy long one contract of April Cattle on August 15.
2. Place a stop equal to 2.5% of the value on the closing price of August 15.
3. Reverse to a short position if that stop is hit. Reverse to be short net 2 contracts.
4. If stopped out after December 1, do not reverse.
5. Liquidate long or short position on December 15.

Cattle prices have almost always staged a year-end rally from December 15 into the first of the year. This trade, to take advantage of this rally, has been correct 92% of the time in 13 years. The trade has produced 1,248 points profit, 640 points loss for a net profit of $2,432.

Trade Rules:

Buy long August cattle on December 15. Use a stop of 120 points from the close of December 15. If the stop is hit, reverse the position to the short side and short twice the amount of the long position. The target on the long side is 2.5% of the close on December 15. If the position reverses to the short side, the target is a straight 200 points.

CATTLE TRADE #5

	Buy Long	Reversal			Target		Profit/ Loss
		Price	Date	Loss	Price	Date	
1964	23.50				24.08	Jan 18	+58
1965	28.35				29.05	Jan 13	+70
1966	28.22				28.92	Jan 9	+70
1967	25.70				26.34	Feb 9	+64
1968	26.95				27.62	Feb 11	+67
1969	31.17				31.94	Mar 5	+77
1970	28.77				29.48	Dec 21	+71
1971	31.80				32.59	Jan 4	+79
1972	38.77				39.73	Dec 26	+96
1973	47.32				48.28	Dec 21	+96
1974	43.32	42.12	Dec 24	-120	40.12	Jan 14	+ 400
1975	42.25				43.25	Jan 28	+ 100
1976	42.25	41.05	Jan 14	-120	43.05	Jan 24	-400

92% CORRECT IN 13 YEARS
1,248 POINTS PROFIT
640 POINTS LOSS
$2,432 NET PROFIT

Rules:
1. Buy long August Cattle on December 15.
2. Set a stop of 120 points below the close on December 15.
3. If stop is hit, reverse the position to the short side and be short twice the amount of the long position.
4. The target is 2.5% of the close on December 15.
5. If you reverse to the short side, the target is a straight 200 points.

It's fascinating to think that during this 14-year time span, this cattle trade needed the reversal factor only one time! That's almost a "sure thing," because the final results showed 12 profits out of 12 trades.

COPPER

It is fitting that an American commodity trader should follow the copper market carefully for two reasons. First, the United States is the world's largest producer of copper; and secondly, the U.S. is also the world's largest consumer of copper.

Other areas where copper is produced are Chile and Peru, as well as the African Congo and Zambia. There is some copper production in the U.S.S.R., but it is difficult to ascertain how reliable the copper production figures are, as well as what the potential untapped copper reserves are behind the Iron Curtain.

A one-cent move in copper is worth $250. Copper is frequently referred to as the red metal, simply because it occasionally looks red. One interesting factor about copper which we do not believe has been discussed by other authorities, is that once copper finds its trend, it usually holds that trend for a long period of time. For those of you who are working on trend following methods in the market, our advice is this: if you find that you have a commodity trend method that is relatively good, you will most likely find that it is even more successful when trading copper.

We have isolated four seasonal tendencies in the copper markets. It is interesting that none of these tendencies have been recorded before and are not those which the standard fundamental authors seek.

COPPER TRADE #1

The first trade has been correct 92% of the time since 1963. This means it has been wrong only once during that time period. It has produced a gain of 88.42 cents with a net loss of 2.35 cents for a dollar value of $21,517. This is one of the most profitable trades in terms of a dollar basis, a risk-reward basis, and percentage of times correct. Obviously traders are going to want to follow this particular tendency.

Trade Rules:

Note the January high for December copper. If prices exceed the January high before March 15, buy long. Sell the long position on April 15.

Let's take an example. In 1963 the January high was 28.87. That price was reached on February 27, at which point the trader would have gone long. On April 15 the price was 29.36; thus, the trader took some 49 points out of the market.

This trade has produced some substantial gains such as in 1964, as well as 1974 and 1976. All in all, it has a remarkable record.

COPPER TRADE #1

	Buy Long	Date	Liquidate April 15	Profit/ Loss
1963	28.87	Feb 27	29.36	+49
1964	31.93	Feb 6	34.68	+275
1965	35.22	Feb 25	41.35	+613
1966	51.80	Feb 1	66.50	+1470
1967	NO TRADE			
1968	47.50	Feb 1	45.15	-235
1969	49.40	Mar 17	51.85	+245
1970	63.90	Feb 3	69.45	+555
1971	49.25	Feb 24	55.75	+650
1972	53.05	Feb 14	53.50	+45
1973	56.65	Feb 1	.65.65	+900
1974	84.90	Feb 4	112.00	+2710
1975	60.60	Feb 13	62.50	+190
1976	61.40	Feb 17	72.80	+1140

92% CORRECT IN 13 YEARS
8842 POINTS PROFIT
235 POINTS LOSS
$21,517 NET PROFIT

Rules:
1. If prices for December copper exceed January highs before March 15, buy long.
2. Liquidate long position April 15.

This trade also attempts to capitalize on the tendency for copper prices to rally in the first part of the year.

This trade has also been correct 93% of the time. It has taken 138.10 cents profit and has had a loss of 4.98 points for a net gain of 146.02 points or some $34,525. This makes it one of the most profitable seasonal trades we have uncovered. It rates extremely well in terms of the risk-reward ratio, etc.

Trade Rules:

The trade rules are simple. Buy September copper on January 19 using a stop that is five percent of the closing price on January 19. If you are stopped out, reverse the position and cover on April 25. Take your profits on the long position on April 15.

Let's take 1967 as an example year. The price on January 19 was 50.35. Five percent of that is 2.51 cents. Subtract 2.51 from 50.35 which gives you a stop at 47.84. Prices reached that price level on February 27, at which point the trader sold short and held the short position until April 25. On April 25, prices were trading at 41.30, so you would have taken out a 654 point profit from that side of the trade leaving the net figure on the positive side for the year of some 400 points.

COPPER TRADE #2

	January 19	5% STOP			Liquidate Long April 15	Liquidate Short April 25	Profit/ Loss
		Date	Price	Loss			
1963	28.81				29.64		+83
1964	31.60				36.60		+500
1965	34.50				46.45		+1195
1966	54.15				73.50		+1935
1967	50.35	Feb 27	47.84	-251		41.30	+654
1968	49.50	Jan 24	47.03	-247		44.70	+233
1969	49.70				55.10		+540
1970	63.30				72.55		+925
1971	46.00				56.25		+1025
1972	50.10				52.65		+255
1973	55.10				67.05		+1195
1974	81.20				116.40		+3520

	January 19	5% STOP			Liquidate Long April 15	Liquidate Short April 25	Profit/ Loss
		Date	Price	Loss			
1975	55.60				60.20		+460
1976	58.80				71.70		+1290

93% CORRECT IN 14 YEARS
13,810 POINTS PROFIT
498 POINTS LOSS
$34,525 NET PROFIT

Rules:
1. Buy September Copper on January 19.
2. Use a stop that is 5% of the closing price on January 19.
3. If stopped out, reverse the position and cover on April 25.
4. Liquidate long position on April 15.

COPPER TRADE #3

This trade goes out for a long-term move, usually lasting more than six months. This is the only capital gains seasonal tendency we were able to isolate in all of our research.

Had the trade rules been followed, one would have had 90.76 cents profit and 7.75 cents loss since 1964. The net gain would have been 83.01 cents or $20,752. The trade was incorrect only one year, 1976.

Trade Rules:

The trade rules tell us that we should buy long January copper if it gets above the April highs. If the high for April occurs the last week of the month, buy on a break above that high or above the high during the first week in May, whichever is higher. Take profits January 15 the following year. Use a stop-loss of ten percent.

If one had followed those elementary procedures, he would have had profits in 1964, 1965, 1966, 1968, 1969, 1970 and 1974. There were no trades in 1967, 1971, 1972, 1973, 1975 or 1976. The 1977 contract resulted in the ten percent stop-loss coming into effect.

Whenever one is going after long-term capital gains in the commodity market, he should be willing to sit through substantial moves in favor of, as well as against, his position. We feel it is extremely significant that we have been able to isolate a capital gains trade in commodities. This simply doesn't happen very often and illustrates the strong seasonal tendency that copper has displayed during this time period.

Just so you can see how a trade works, let's take the trade that occurred in 1965. The high for April was 37.10. That price was not exceeded until September 3 of 1965 when prices reached that level. You should have purchased at that point and held the position until the following January 15 when prices were 40.60. The net gain here was 3.50 cents.

COPPER TRADE #3

	Buy Long	Date	Liquidate Jan 15	Profit/ Loss
1964	29.49	May 10	31.50	+201
1965	37.10	Sep 3	40.60	+350
1966	45.35	July 27	61.70	+1635
1967	NO TRADE			
1968	42.10	May 22	67.30	+2520
1969	45.95	Sep 16	52.70	+675
1970	55.35	June 2	70.70	+1535
1971	NO TRADE			
1972	NO TRADE			
1973	NO TRADE			
1974	67.90	May 22	89.50	+2160
1975	NO TRADE			
1976	NO TRADE			
1977	77.90	July 1		-775

93% CORRECT IN 14 YEARS
9,076 POINTS PROFIT
775 POINTS LOSS
$20,752 NET PROFIT

Rules:

1. Buy long January Copper if it gets above the April highs. If the high for April occurs the last week in April, buy on a break above that high or above the high the first week in May whichever is the higher of the two.
2. Use a stop of 10% of the buy price.
3. Take profits January 15 the following year.

Profits for this trade were 67.15 cents, minus a loss of 11.50 cents for a net profit of 55.65 cents or $13,913. This is not the best seasonal tendency trade for copper, but it has made a decent amount of money and the win-loss ratio of 6:1 qualifies it as being of interest to all traders.

Trade Rules:

Sell short September copper if prices trade below the lowest low of the previous two weeks starting April 1. Liquidate the position on July 1. Use a stop that is one price tick above the highest inter-day high obtained by the copper contract prior to your selling short.

This trade has been consistent; however, when it loses, it loses for a pretty hefty chunk. Notice that in 1976 there was a 430 point loss, in 1973 a 395 point loss and in 1969 a 325 point loss.

Obviously, this trade is not for the poorly margined or weak at heart commodity trader. Yet, the figures as presented here certainly do indicate the tendency, and it is a strong one. This, of course, is sympathetic with the rally in copper which we see in the first part of the year. At some point, that rally must subside. Our work indicates that these selling pressures are to occur sometime in April. What we have done is put in a screening factor, realizing prices will start to decline sometime in the April-May time period. However, we have put in a requirement that prices must fall below the lowest low of the last two weeks or ten days before we want to enter the short side of the market and acknowledge a potential trend reversal.

COPPER TRADE #4

	Sell Short	Date	STOP Price	Date	Loss	Liquidate July 1	Profit/ Loss
1965	44.25	Apr 29				42.80	+145
1966	72.50	Apr 18				69.95	+255
1967	43.75	Apr 3				42.35	+140
1968	46.25	Apr 17				44.50	+175
1969	54.60	Apr 30				57.85	-325
1970	71.25	Apr 21				62.00	+925
1971	56.15	Apr 26				50.05	+610
1972	52.90	Apr 13				47.55	+535

	Sell Short	Date	STOP Price	STOP Date	STOP Loss	Liquidate July 1	Profit/ Loss
1973	65.80	May 2	69.75	May 21	-395		
1974	123.40	May 13				89.40	+3400
1975	61.40	Apr 7				56.10	+530
1976	71.60	May 3				75.90	-430

75% CORRECT IN 12 YEARS
6715 POINTS PROFIT
1150 POINTS LOSS
$13,913 NET PROFIT

Rules:

1. Sell Short September copper if it trades below the lowest low of the previous two weeks starting April 1.
2. Use a stop that is one price tick above the highest inter-day high obtained by the copper contract prior to your selling short.
3. Liquidate the position on July 1.

CORN

When it comes to finding and establishing seasonal tendencies in the corn market, we have been able to isolate three very reliable tendencies. This is interesting when one considers that some of the leading authors of commodities have said, "In corn, speculators exert a contra-seasonal force which has, except for carrying charges, virtually eliminated seasonal fluctuations."

We think you will agree from the data to be presented, there are strong seasonal tendencies in the trading patterns for corn. As most people know, the U.S. produces more corn than any other country. Beyond that, we also process more corn than all the other countries combined. There are many uses for corn, an important one being for animal feed. Corn can be used and processed wet or dry. The process "wet" is used primarily for sugars and starches. The process "dry" can be used for oils and animal or human consumption. There is also some use of corn for alcohol and corn liquor, as well as for beer and breakfast food.

In recent years corn production has begun to increase, which may be forecasting what's in store. During the 1965 to 1970 time period, corn production had not increased much, but now we have seen a higher production due to higher yield per acre. The corn belt in the United States is in the mid-west in the Iowa, Illinois and Minnesota areas.

There are several government reports which help the corn trader. The most important one might be the Feed Situation Report and/or Planting Intentions and Crop Production reports.

CORN TRADE #1

This trade is based on corn prices declining in mid to late January and into February of each year. The trade has been 93% correct since 1963. This means that it has only had one loss in the last 14 years of trading. We think that record certainly demonstrates the seasonal tendency of this market. The gross gain was 53.5 cents, net loss was 1.4 cents and the profit was 52.1 cents for a total of $2,605.

Trade Rules:

Sell short one contract of December corn on January 18. Take a profit of 2.5% of the entry price. If the target is not hit, liquidate the last trading day in February.

The trade has not produced spectacular sums of dollars in terms of its performance; however, it has been reliable, especially considering the fact that there has been only one bad trade in 14 years. On a win-loss ratio the trade looks very good in that the only loss was for less than two cents and the average profit for the trade has been 4.1¢. There was a high profit in 1975 of 8.0 cents and the lowest profit ever was 3.0 cents in 1963. So on the risk-reward ratio basis, considering the inactivity of the corn market, this certainly is a trade that's going to rate right up there in the trader's notebook.

CORN TRADE #1

	Sell Short Jan 18	Target	Date Target Reached	February 28 Liquidation Price	Profit in Points
1963	118.3	115.4	Feb 4		3.0
1964	122.6	119.6	Feb 13		3.0
1965	128.8	125.6		130.2	-1.4
1966	131.3	128.1	Feb 18		3.2
1967	142.2	138.7	Feb 16		3.5
1968	123.3	120.3		121.6	1.7
1969	120.7	117.7	Feb 25		3.0
1970	125.1	122.0	Feb 4		3.1
1971	159.2	155.3	Feb 1		3.9
1972	124.6	121.3		121.5	3.1
1973	148.8	145.1	Feb 8		3.7
1974	293.0	285.7	Jan 23		7.3
1975	322.0	314.0	Jan 20		8.0
1976	279.2	270.2	Jan 26		7.0

Rules:
1. Sell short one contract of December corn on January 18.
2. Take a profit of 2.5% of the entry price.
3. If the target of 2.5% of the entry price is not hit, liquidate the last trading day in February.

CORN TRADE #2

In studying the charts we found that there is a strong influence in corn prices to rally starting in October. We searched and searched and tried many different methods to ferret out this trade and finally established trade rules that have worked quite well.

The trade has produced 139.1 cents profit; 2.3 cents loss for a net profit of 136.8 cents and a dollar gain of $6,840. It has been correct 92% of the time. While we have seen 92% accuracy, the overall tendency for prices to rally starting in mid-October has existed 72% of the time. There were three years when there were reversals in the market and we reversed to take advantage of the turn.

Trade Rules:

Buy long December corn on October 14, using a 10-point stop. If your stop is hit, reverse your position, being short twice the amount you were long. Take a ten-point profit on the short sale. Liquidate your long position on December 15.

The trade has produced some substantial profits in the 1970's, particularly in the 1973-1976 time period. Nonetheless, it was equally profitable in the 1960's when corn was not actively traded.

CORN TRADE #2

	Buy Long Oct 14	10-POINT REVERSAL			LIQUIDATE AT 10-PT. TARGET ON REVERSAL		Liquidate Long On Dec 15	Profit (Points)
		Price	Date	Loss In Points	Price	Date		
1963	116.7						118.0	1.3
1964	120.7						122.3	1.6
1965	114.6						124.0	9.4
1966	135.0						140.0	5.0
1967	114.5						114.6	0.1
1968	105.3						114.8	9.5
1969	119.3						117.0	-2.3
1970	148.5						150.1	1.6
1971	114.3						118.6	4.3
1972	133.2						159.5	26.3
1973	253.5	243.5	Oct 15	-10.0	233.5	Oct 30		20.0
1974	388.0	378.0	Oct 17	-10.0	368.0	Oct 25		20.0
1975	296.2	286.2	Oct 21	-10.0	276.2	Oct 27		20.0
1976	271.0	261.0	Oct 22	-10.0	251.0	Oct 29		20.0

92% CORRECT SINCE 1963
139.1 POINTS PROFIT
2.3 POINTS LOSS
$6,840 NET PROFIT

Rules:
1. Buy long December Corn on October 14.
2. Use a 10-point stop.
3. If your stop is hit, reverse your position being short twice the amount of contracts you were long.
4. Take a ten-point profit on the short sale.
5. Liquidate the long position on December 15.

In studying the chart, as well as our information from our massive computer data bank, we notice there is a tendency for the December contract to decline in the late summer or early fall of the year. During the last 17 years, the trade has been incorrect only three times which means it has been correct 83% of the time.

The trade has produced 67.3 cents profit, 18.7 cents loss for a net profit of $2,430.

Trade Rules:

Sell short one contract of December corn on September 1 from 1960 to 1969. Starting 1970, sell short one contract of December corn on September 15. Liquidate the short position on September 30. Use a straight 10-point stop.

CORN TRADE #3

	Sell Short Sept 1	Sell Short Sept 15	10-Point Stop		Liquidate Short Sept 30	Profit/ Loss
			Date Stopped Out	Price		
1960	110.5				108.5	+2.0
1961	114.0				108.5	+5.5
1962	106.0				105.0	+1.0
1963	113.6				119.8	-6.2
1964	120.8				120.6	+.2
1965	118.3				116.3	+2.0
1966	147.2				138.1	+9.1
1967	117.2				113.3	+3.9
1968	103.2				101.5	+1.7
1969	116.8				115.3	+1.5
1970		155.7			149.5	+6.2
1971		115.1			112.8	+2.3
1972		143.2			140.5	+2.7
1973		259.7			252.5	+7.2
1974		340.7		350.7		-10.0
1975		300.7			303.2	-2.5
1976		288.5			266.5	+22.0

Rules:
1. Sell short one contract of December Corn on September 1 (from 1960 to 1969).
   Sell short one contract of December Corn on September 15 (from 1970 to 1976).
2. Use a straight 10-point stop.
3. Liquidate the short position on September 30.

CORN TRADE #4

This trade has been 64% correct for the last 14 years with a gain of 106.8 cents, a loss of 30.9 cents and a dollar gain of $3,795.

Trade Rules:

Check prices of December corn on April 15 and again on May 15. If prices are higher on May 15, buy long; if they are lower, sell short.

Take profits or losses on the long position July 1. Take the profits or losses on the short position July 30. Use a straight 10-point stop.

CORN TRADE #4

	Prices on Apr 15	Buy Long May 15	Sell Short May 15	Stopped Out Using 10-Point Stop	Liquidate Long July 1	Liquidate Short July 30	Profit/ Loss
1963	113.3	115.7			123.0		+7.3
1964	121.8		117.7			117.1	+.6
1965	121.0		119.6			120.0	− 4
1966	120.6	121.5			137.7		+16.2
1967	138.8		135.6			121.6	+14.0
1968	121.2		119.6			105.7	+13.9

	Prices on Apr 15	Buy Long May 15	Sell Short May 15	Stopped Out Using 10-Point Stop	Liquidate Long July 1	Liquidate Short July 30	Profit/ Loss
1969	117.5	124.6			124.6		0
1970	119.7	121.5			132.3		+10.8
1971	147.2		137.2	147.2			-10.0
1972	129.0		125.8			126.3	-.5
1973	153.3	171.0			202.0		+31.0
1974	251.7		240.5	250.5			-10.0
1975	256.2		244.2	254.2			-10.0
1976	267.0	270.0			283.0		+13.0

64% CORRECT IN 14 YEARS
106.8 POINTS PROFIT
30.9 POINTS LOSS
$3,795 NET PROFIT

Rules:
1. Check prices of December corn on April 15 and on May 15.
2. If prices are higher on May 15 than on April 15, buy one contract.
3. If prices are lower on May 15 than April 15, sell one contract.
4. Use a straight 10-point stop.
5. Take profits or losses on the long position on July 1.
6. Take profits or losses on the short position on July 30.

COTTON

Unfortunately, we could find only one trade for cotton that we felt was worthy of presentation to the reader. We did a great deal of work on the cotton market trying to seek out an advisable seasonal tendency in the market. There are several; however, they come into and out of phase in the market too much to be feasible.

COTTON TRADE #1

The trade has been wrong only three times since 1963, which means during the 14-year time period, it has been correct 79% of the time. The trade has produced 42.51 cents profit and 1.54 cents loss for a net 40.97 cents or a dollar gain of $20,485. The dollar gain here is quite substantial and is due in part to the volatility we have seen in the cotton market. The trade attempts to capitalize on the seasonal tendency for prices to rally during the summer months, particularly June and July.

Trade Rules:

The rules are simple. Buy long December cotton on June l and liquidate that long position on July 22.

Let's take 1970 as an example. In 1970 the closing price on June 1 was 26.15. The closing price on July 22 was 26.18 for a net gain of three points on the trade. No big deal. However, in 1973 the closing price on June 1 was 47.99 and on July 22 was 61.70 for a net gain of 13.71 or some $6,855. The most spectacular year for the seasonal tendency was 1973; nonetheless, the tendency has been correct for the last four years and all years have produced rather substantial profits.

We tried many other ways to ascertain a seasonal tendency in the cotton market, and unfortunately, were not able to come up with anything we felt qualified for consideration. Therefore, we have only this one seasonal tendency trade in the cotton market at this time.

COTTON TRADE #1

	Buy Long June 1	Liquidate July 22	Profit/ Loss
1963	32.53	32.86	+.33
1964	28.80	31.15	+2.35
1965	29.95	29.63	-.32
1966	21.75	22.22	+.47
1967	26.75	29.78	+3.03
1968	31.06	33.25	+2.19
1969	25.82	25.65	-.17
1970	26.15	26.18	+.03
1971	29.40	32.04	+2.64
1972	30.55	29.49	-1.05
1973	47.99	61.70	+13.71
1974	50.35	56.05	+5.70
1975	45.77	49.13	+3.36
1976	67.30	76.00	+8.70

79% CORRECT SINCE 1963
4251 POINTS PROFIT
154 POINTS LOSS
$20,485 NET PROFIT

Rules:
1. Buy long December Cotton on June 1.
2. Liquidate position on July 22.

EGGS

When it comes to eggs, perhaps the best advice one can give to the inexperienced trader is this: *Don't trade eggs.*

That's right. Eggs are one of the most volatile commodities and, if any of the commodities are manipulated, eggs are. There probably has been more public money lost in trading eggs than any other single commodity, judging from the traders whom we have talked with throughout the country.

This is not to say that there are not opportunities trading eggs. *(I can recall one time when I ran an account of some $3,000 up to almost $75,000 in approximately three months basically trading the egg market. LRW)*

There are three extremely strong seasonal tendencies in eggs, in fact, these are perhaps the strongest seasonal tendencies that we were able to locate. Before getting into those tendencies, let's talk a little about the egg market so that you'll know what you're getting into should you decide to trade eggs.

In the late 1960's came the research quetioning the relationship between egg consumption and cholesterol. It's almost automatic when one person mentions eggs for someone else to mention cholesterol. Nonetheless, as to the cholesterol scare (which may or may not be real when dealing with eggs) there is plenty of evidence to show that even heavy consumption of eggs may not increase the cholesterol level. In fact, the body's natural agent to combat cholesterol is lecithen. Lecithen is found in egg yolks and many studies have been done which indicate a high consumption of eggs without a high consumption of fatty meats does not increase cholesterol levels.

If you were a producer of eggs, the figures most relevant to you would be the number of eggs which a bird lays per month (19 to 20 per month is good production) and your cost per dozen (which at current price levels is about 25¢ to 27¢) for the eggs you would "manufacture" in your egg-laying farm.

67

The business of laying eggs is an extremely scientific business compared to yesteryear when eggs were produced in a most random fashion. In fact, it is now possible to extend the egg laying years of a bird. This is done by starving the bird to the point where it starts to lose its feathers, then force feeding the bird. This unusual dietary action, for some reason, increases the bird's production from one to two years.

Eggs are traded on the Chicago Mercantile Exchange. One contract represents 22,500 dozen eggs, or one carload. One of the problems in trading is that taking delivery of eggs is rather unusual; thus, if you are long eggs as they are expiring, it is extremely important to know what chances you have of being delivered. A hard and fast rule says that you do not want to take delivery of eggs *under any circumstance, in any way whatsoever, at any time!*

If there is any indication that you may have to take delivery on eggs, and you can tell this by delivery dates, notices, etc., then you should simply exit the market.

The USDA releases a "Poultry and Egg Situation" four or five times a year to give current statistics concerning the supply of eggs in the United States. Incidently, the U.S. is the world's largest producer of eggs with current production of 76 billion. If you decide to trade eggs, the type of eggs you will be trading are graded Large A eggs. So the next time you are in the supermarket, you might want to look at the Large A eggs, not the AAA or AA or King Size or Small Size, but the Large A eggs. These are the ones you are going to be trading.

By and large, civilian consumption and production of eggs go pretty much hand in hand. If you were to make an astute study of the production of eggs, you would find that production tends to be higher during the first part of the year, particularly in the March-April-May time period. It then slacks off and declines in the August-September-October time period.

This is pretty much what happens with the consumption of eggs as well, which is especially interesting, because as you will see from the three seasonal trades presented here, the best trade for the long side is to buy during April which is when the production of eggs is up the highest, and the best short selling opportunity comes in September when the production of eggs, as well as the consumption of eggs, has declined.

OK. Let's start with the first seasonal egg trade--one that has never been wrong in the last 14 years of market activity.

During the last 14 years, the trade presented below has shown a total profit of $18,490 (excluding commission costs).

This is an incredible trade, one that has been right 14 times out of 14 times. This is most unusual and deserves a trader's close attention. It also reiterates the validity of seasonal trading.

Trade Rules:

This trade requires extremely simple rules. All one needed to have done during the past 14 years to make the $18,490 was to have purchased two contracts of September eggs the first Friday in April. You would then set two targets. Your first target would be that, once prices have advanced 5% from the buy price, liquidate. You would liquidate the second contract on the 15th day of July.

To arrive at 5% for the liquidation of the first contract, you would take 5% and multiply it by the buy price. As an example, in 1963 the price of September eggs the first trading day in April was 33.35. Multiply that figure by 5% and you will get 1.66¢. Add 1.66¢ to 33.35 to arrive at a profit of 35.01 which means you would be selling at 35.01 which occurred on the 10th day in June. The second contract you would simply have liquidated on the 15th trading day in July.

We have not developed stop points or reversal points in this trade because it has always been successful. Nonetheless, a trader entering the trade would want some kind of protection and we would suggest a stop equal to the amount you are trading for. In other words, use 5% as your minimum downside risk. However, considering the validity of the trade, it would not surprise us if one could trade this without a stop

EGG TRADE #1

	1st Friday in April	5% TARGET			Liquidate July 15	Profit	Net Profit
		Price	Date	Profit			
1963	33.35	35.01	June 10	166	34.45	110	+276
1964	32.25	33.86	June 16	161	34.65	240	+401
1965	32.65	34.28	Apr 19	163	33.80	115	+278
1966	34.80	36.54	June 14	174	39.00	420	+594
1967	35.35	37.11	May 15	176	35.35	0	+176
1968	36.70	38.58	Apr 23	188	39.90	320	+508

69

	1st Friday in April	5% TARGET			Liquidate July 15	Profit	Net Profit
		Price	Date	Profit			
1969	37.50	39.37	Apr 17	187	44.25	675	+862
1970	34.95	36.69	May 22	174	39.85	490	+664
1971	37.35	39.21	May 11	186	37.70	35	+221
1972	39.00	40.95	May 9	195	37.80	-120	+75
1973	53.85	56.54	May 8	269	70.45	1660	+1929
1974	50.15	52.65	Apr 15	250	54.20	405	+655
1975	50.90	53.44	Apr 10	254	53.05	215	+469
1976	51.00	53.55	Apr 30	255	59.55	855	+1110

100% CORRECT IN 14 YEARS
8218 POINTS PROFIT
$18,490 NET PROFIT

Rules:
1. Buy long two contracts of September eggs the first Friday in April.
2. Set two targets:
   a. Liquidate one contract when prices have advanced 5%.
   b. Liquidate the second contract on July 15.
3. Use a stop equal to the amount of the target.

This is a most incredible trade when you study the number of times in the last 14 years that prices have literally skyrocketed during the month of April. What we have tried to do is make certain that the trade always got some profit out with our 5% target and then also had a free ride for an additional profit, should the market move higher, using the closing price on July 15 as our second point to liquidate and take profits. This seemed to work quite well and, in some years, took substantial profits such as in 1966, 1968, 1969 and 1976.

EGG TRADE #2

This trade is also a buy long trade—one that has not been quite as spectacular in terms of percentage times it was right or wrong during the last 14 years. Nevertheless, the trade should certainly not be overlooked inasmuch as it has taken a profit of $10,141 during the last 14 years.

70

The trade has been right 65% of the time which means there were five years when the trade did not show a net profit for the year. The cluster of these years in 1971, 1972, 1973 was the worst time period the trade had.

On this particular trade, though it is not as reliable as the first trade, it is interesting to note that because it was correct some 65% of the time, it made approximately $3 for every $1 it lost. This certainly is not a bad risk-reward ratio.

Trade Rules:

To initiate this trade, you buy long two contracts of September eggs on the third day in August. If August 3 is a Saturday or Sunday, then buy on the following Monday. Set a straight stop which is equal to 5% of your price on the entry day. As an example, if the price was 58.45 as it was in 1976, you would have a stop of 292 points subtracted from 58.45, or a straight stop of 55.53.

Set a target to sell one of your long positions at 10% of the price of August 3. In other words, again using 1976 as an example, if the price were 58.45, you would add 5.84 points to achieve a target of 64.29. That price was attained on August 27 and you took your profit of 584 points.

The final rule is that after September 1, you will want to use a trailing stop. To do this, you simply place a stop in the market every day. This stop is determined by noticing the lowest low of the last 4 days and placing your stop at that level. In other words, prior to a market opening, go back and notice the lowest low traded during the previous four days and use that price as a straight stop in the market. If prices hold above there, you are, of course, still long and will continue the procedure the next day. If prices fall below that price, you are stopped out near that price.

That's all the rules there are to that trade. It is a relatively simple trade to take and again has an extraordinary batting average, especially considering the high volatility of the egg market.

EGG TRADE #2

	Buy Long Aug 3	10% TARGET			TRAILING STOP AFTER 9 - 1			Net Profit
		Price	Date	Profit	Price	Date	Profit	
1963	33.70				34.85	Sept 11	+115	+230
1964	35.40				35.65	Sept 14	+25	+50
1965	31.85				30.26	Sept 1	-159	-318
1966	39.50	43.45	Sept 1	+395	47.55	Sept 19	+805	+1200
1967	34.20				32.49	Aug 11	-171	-342
1968	35.15	38.66	Aug 13	+351	44.05	Sept 16	+890	+1241
1969	43.30				46.45	Sept 16	+315	+630
1970	37.55	41.30	Aug 11	+375	43.60	Aug 21	+605	+980
1971	39.40				37.43	Aug 16	-197	-394
1972	33.40				31.73	Aug 7	-167	-334
1973	79.65				75.67	Aug 17	-398	-796
1974	49.00	53.90	Aug 14	+496	55.35	Aug 26	+635	+1131
1975	54.25				55.20	Sept 9	+95	+190
1976	58.45	64.29	Aug 27	+584	63.00	Sept 2	+455	+1039

65% CORRECT IN 14 YEARS
6,691 POINTS PROFIT
2,184 POINTS LOSS
$10,141 NET PROFIT

Rules:
1. Buy long 2 contracts of September Eggs on the 3rd day of August.
   (If August 3 is a Saturday or Sunday, then buy on the following Monday.)
2. Use a straight stop equal to 5% of your price on entry day.
3. Set two targets:
   a. Liquidate one contract when prices have advanced 10%.
   b. Use a trailing stop that is the low of the previous 4 market days after September 1.
4. If 10% target is not reached by September 1, use a trailing stop that is the low of the previous 4 market days for both contracts.

Another seasonal tendency trade is one that involves a seasonal tendency for the price of eggs to decline from about September 15 to about October 15.

This is another dynamite trade that has been 100% correct producing profits in all of the last 14 years. It is of particular interest to note that this trade has been the most successful in terms of gross dollars of the egg market, with profits of $33,999 during that 14 years.

Trade Rules:

Sell two contracts of November eggs on the close of September 15. If September 14 is a Friday, sell on Monday's opening. Cover one contract on the close of the market on October 15 and then cover the other contract any time that prices close higher than the highest close of the previous week. Stop and reverse (buy long 4 contracts being long net 2 contracts) if prices move 5% above the price on September 15.

Like the previous two egg trades, the rules are relatively simple because the seasonal tendency is that strong.

EGG TRADE #3

	Sell Short Sept 15	Exit One Contract on October 15		Liquidate 2nd Contract			Net Profit
		Price	Profit	Date	Price	Profit	
1963	35.60	35.05	+55	Nov 21	31.00	+460	+515
1964	34.25	32.90	+135	Nov 20	27.05	+720	+855
1965	33.20	29.65	+355	Nov 1	30.65	+255	+610
1966	40.15	36.40	+375	Oct 17	36.80	+335	+710
1967	35.60	28.25	+735	Oct 23	29.10	+650	+1385
1968	44.55	40.85	+370	Oct 23	38.90	+565	+935
1969	44.30	*R1		*R1			+3296
1970	39.30	+36.60	+270	Oct 20	36.90	+240	+510
1971	35.70	+35.15	+55	Nov 8	28.25	+745	+800
1972	43.25	+31.05	+1220	Oct 20	32.00	+1125	+2345

	Sell Short Sept 15	Exit One Contract on October 15		Liquidate 2nd Contract			Net Profit
		Price	Profit	Date	Price	Profit	
1973	61.35	+56.80	+455	Oct 26	58.25	+310	+765
1974	61.30	+56.25	+505	Nov 12	50.80	+1050	+1555
1975	56.00	+54.20	+180	Oct 27	54.20	+180	+360
1976	60.30	*R2		*R2			+470

100% CORRECT IN 13 YEARS
15,111 POINTS PROFIT
$33,999 NET PROFIT

*R1 Short @ 44.30. Reversed to long side @ 46.51 on October 10 for a -221 on 2 contracts. Liquidated 2 long contracts @ 65.20 on November 20 for a profit of 18.69 x 2 for a total of 37.38 cents profit.

*R2 Short @60.30. Reversed to long side @ 63.50 on October 7 for a -320 on 2 contracts. Liquidated 2 long contracts @ 69.05 on November 17 for a profit of 11.10 cents.

Rules:
1. Sell two contracts of November eggs on the close of September 15. If September 14 is a Friday, sell on Monday's opening.
2. Use a stop that is 5% of the September 15 price. If stop is hit, reverse to the long side with 2 contracts and use 5% of purchase price as stop.
3. Cover one contract on the close of October 15.
4. Cover one contract any time prices close higher than the highest close of the previous week.

Egg Commentary

In reviewing these figures, we noticed an interesting thing. These three trades alone made a profit of $62,630 over 13½ years. Dividing this by 13.5, means there is a net profit of some $4,473 per year if one had simply traded eggs on a seasonal tendency through the rules given above. Obviously, there is not assurance that these trades will work as successfully in the future, but the general feeling given by the figures is that there are three very strong seasonal tendencies in the egg market and we have been able to isolate these with some degree of regularity.

There are probably additional seasonal tendencies in the egg market but we have not been able to ferret out a successful trading program for them.

74

For sure, if one is an egg trader, or is remotely interested in trading this market, he would not want to be bucking the trends of the three time periods: (1) Buying in the first part of the year; (2) Buying again during the summer months; and (3) Selling in the middle of September.

We would also imagine a seasonal egg trader could make the above results more spectacular in trading into delivery and contract expiration as the egg market has been known to go absolutely wild in the last seven to eight trading sessions.

FLAX

The seasonal tendency we isolated for flax has been correct 86% of the time. Not many American commodity traders follow the flax market, so we have not devoted a great deal of attention to the fundamentals; however, we did devote a considerable amount of time trying to discover good seasonal trades in the flax market. Unfortunately, we only found one.

For the 14 years traded, we show 935.9 points profit, 3.51 points loss, 900.8 cents net profit with a dollar amount of $45,040 on a 10,000 bushel lot.

Trade Rules:

Buy December flax on the first trading day in May. If prices are lower on July 1, sell short, liquidating the short position July 31. If prices are higher on July 1, hold until July 15. If prices are lower on July 15, sell; if prices are higher on July 15, hold and liquidate on July 31.

Prices for 1975 were not available.

FLAX TRADE #1

	Prices on May 1	Prices on July 1	Loss on Reversal	Prices on July 15	Liquidate on July 15	Liquidate on July 31	Profit/ Loss
1963	331.1	326.2	-4.9	322.5		314.1	+12.1
1964	318.0	321.0		324.0		337.0	+19.0
1965	325.0	316.0	-9.0	310.5		311.0	+5.0
1966	300.7	301.5		302.2		302.2	+1.5
1967	308.5	311.6		346.2		349.5	+41.0
1968	341.5	333.3	-8.2	330.0		320.2	+13.1
1969	287.1	292.2		288.5	+1.4	285.2	0
1970	268.7	259.7	-9.0	265.2		260.7	-1.0
1971	251.0	248.0	-3.0	246.3		239.7	+8.3
1972	267.0	281.2		287.0		284.5	+17.5
1973	483.0	691.0		764.0		964.0	+481.0
1974	851.0	892.0		1003.0		1131.0	+280.0
1975							
1976	657.0	759.0		763		713.0	+56.0

86% CORRECT IN 13 YEARS
935.9 POINTS PROFIT
35.1 POINTS LOSS
$45.040 NET PROFIT

Rules:
1. Buy December Flaxseed on the first trading day in May.
2. If prices are lower on July 1, sell short and liquidate on July 31.
3. If prices are higher on July 1, hold until July 15.
4. If prices are lower on July 15, sell.
5. If prices are higher on July 15, hold and liquidate on July 31.

HOGS

In seeking out seasonal tendency trades for the hog market, one must realize that hogs have not been trading for a great length of time. In fact, they began trading in February, 1966, so we do not have as long a track record to study in the hog market as we do in other markets.

It takes approximately 200 days, that is between 170 and 200 days, for a hog to reach maturation at which point it is slaughtered. At that time it should weigh between 210 and 225 pounds.

The hog will slaughter out at about 220 pounds, which means it has been fed approximately 440 to 500 pounds of grain because it takes two pounds of grain to put one pound of meat on a hog. About 18% of the animal will be used for ham. The production of hogs is dependent to a great deal on what happens with the price of corn. For this reason, of course, most hogs are grown in the corn belt area of the United States. If a trader is going to follow hogs closely, he would also have to follow the price of corn.

According to one study over the last 80 years, the average length of a hog cycle has been four years. That is, it takes four years to go from one high to the next high or four years to go from one low to the next low. During the fifty-five years from 1890 to 1945, there were some sixteen hog cycles of this approximate duration.

A high price for hogs one year, just as a high price for any commodity, will increase production which means we tend to see prices lower the following year because there are too many people producing in the market. We were able to isolate four hog market trades, three of which were 100% correct.

The first trade is one of the strongest seasonal tendencies in the market operating in hogs as well as pork bellies. Since 1966, the trade has been correct 100% of the time and there has been a trade every year. The net gain has been 14.81 cents which means a total dollar profit of $4,443.

Trade Rules:

The trade rules are to buy long on the close of the first trading day in November. Establish a target that is 5% of the closing price of that day at which point one would take profits. Use a stop that is equal to 2.5 percent of the low of November 1. If you have not closed out the position by the last day in March, close out the last trading day in March.

Let's follow a trade through to completion to see what would have happened. In 1967 the closing price of April hogs on the first trading day in November was 19 cents. The price never rallied 5% of the value—which would have .95 cents added to 19 cents or 19.95 cents. That price (19.95) was never reached. However, on the last trading day in March, prices were 19.35 at which point we would have liquidated the long position and taken a profit of .35 cents. Most of the time the target has been reached immediately, sometimes in early November or usually by mid-December. If prices are not reached by that time, simply hold on until the last trading day in March.

The fact that this trade has been 100% correct argues well for its ability to continue operating in the future.

HOG TRADE #1

	1st Trading Day in Nov	5% TARGET		Liquidate Last Trading Day in March		Profit/ Loss
		Date	Price	Date	Price	
1966	21.15	Nov 17	22.20			+105
1967	19.00			Mar 29	19.35	+35
1968	18.25	Feb 10	19.16			+91
1969	24.10	Nov 10	25.30			+120

	1st Trading Day in Nov	5% TARGET		Liquidate Last Trading Day in March		Profit/ Loss
		Date	Price	Date	Price	
1970	17.67	Nov 17	18.55			+88
1971	21.40	Nov 15	22.47			+107
1972	26.67	Dec 11	28.00			+133
1973	44.77	Nov 9	47.00			+223
1974	42.35	Nov 6	44.46			+211
1975	43.82	Nov 5	46.01			+219
1976	29.95	Nov 8	31.44			+149

100% CORRECT IN 11 YEARS
14.81 POINTS PROFIT
$4,443 NET PROFIT

Rules:
1. Buy long April Hogs at the closing price the first trading day in November.
2. Use a stop that is equal to 2.5% of the low of the November prices.
3. The target is 5% of the closing price of the day you bought long.
4. If the position has not been closed out by the last trading day in March, close out the position.

HOG TRADE #2

The next seasonal trade for hogs occurs because there is a tendency for prices to establish an important turning point in April of each year. Apparently there are factors influencing the production of hogs and during April of each year these factors tend to cause a trend reversal point. We can identify this point in several ways and the one our records showed as the best is presented here.

The trade has taken out 32.95 cents since 1970--as far back as we have records on the August contract, which means there was a net profit of $9,885. Again, the trade was 100% correct.

Trade Rules:

Check the price of August Hogs on March 1. If prices are higher on April 1 than on March 1, buy long. If prices are lower on April 1, sell short. If short, liquidate the

81

position on June 15. If long, liquidate the position on June 15.

Theoretically, if one had followed these rules during the last seven years, he would have shown profits every single year. The profits were substantial in 1964, 1965 and decent in 1973 and 1976. The only marginal year was 1971 when hog action only produced a gain of .70 cents. What is interesting is that we have apparently isolated an important turning point in the spring of the year that is based on what prices do from the first day in March to the first day in April. Hog traders will want to watch this time period carefully.

HOG TRADE #2

	March 1	April 1		June 15	Profit/ Loss
1970	27.55	25.10	(sell short)	23.47	+163
1971	20.65	21.95	(buy long)	22.65	+70
1972	25.67	27.07	(buy long)	28.37	+130
1973	34.22	34.90	(buy long)	40.17	+527
1974	44.40	38.85	(sell short)	25.02	+1383
1975	39.65	45.20	(buy long)	51.77	+657
1976	42.22	44.25	(buy long)	47.90	+365

100% CORRECT IN 7 YEARS
32.95 POINTS PROFIT
$9,885 NET PROFIT

Rules:
1. If prices are higher for August Hogs on April 1 than on March 1, buy long.
2. If prices are lower for August Hogs on April 1 than on March 1, sell short.
3. Liquidate position on June 15.

HOG TRADE #3

The next seasonal trade has also been 100% correct; however, we should advise you that it only has been in operation two of the last seven trading years.

The trade has produced a net gain of 8.25 cents for a total profit of $2,475. The reason we are putting the trade in despite its limited appearance, is that the trade rules are so tight we suspect that if the trade rules are met, one is well on his way to profits, and we want to establish this as a seasonal tendency which operates for a rally in the hog market.

Trade Rules:

The trade rules are simple. Note the high for the October contract in July. If after August 20, the high has been penetrated, buy long. Take your profits October 15.

This trade works, we suspect, because of the fact that prices tend to decline during the August time period. However, if prices do a reversal here by going above the July high (this would be an abnormal event) we want to be long.

HOG TRADE #3

	Price	Date	Oct 15	Profit/ Loss
1970	NO TRADE			
1971	NO TRADE			
1972	27.37	Aug 24	29.42	+205
1973	NO TRADE			
1974	NO TRADE			
1975	51.90	Aug 20	58.10	+620
1976	NO TRADE			

100% CORRECT IN 7 YEARS
825 POINTS PROFIT
$2,475 NET PROFIT

Rules:
1. If the July high of October hogs is penetrated after August 20, buy long.
2. Take profits on October 15.

HOG TRADE #4

This trade is based on the apparent tendency for hog prices to decline during the summer months. There are some fundamental reasons why this should happen. The main one is that there is less demand for hogs at this time period. During the summer months we tend to see lighter meals served and less meat consumed especially meats such as bacon and pork. The main meat items used for summer eating are barbeque items such as chicken and beef; since pork is not consumed as heavily at this time, the tendency is for prices to decline.

Since 1970 the trade has been 100% correct if all the rules had been followed. However, for three of those years, one had to reverse, suffering a loss, before profits were eventually obtained. Nonetheless, the profit has been 50.57 cents with a net loss of 3.00 cents for a total profit of 47.57 cents which is $14,271 profit. Not bad, considering the results are from the lackluster hog market.

Trade Rules:

Sell short August hogs the first trading day in July. Use a 100 point stop above that closing price. If the stop is hit, reverse being long twice the amount you shorted. Liquidate the long position August 1. Liquidate the short position August 15.

It should be pointed out that the only data we have from 1967 to 1969 is on charts and on that information, 1967 was a down year and it would have worked; 1968 was a down year and it would have worked; 1969 prices rallied and the position would have been reversed; however, the trade would have worked. Thus, we really have ten years of data that suggest we have isolated one more exceptionally strong seasonal tendency rule.

HOG TRADE #4

| | July 1 | 100-Point Reversal | | | Liquidate Short Aug 15 | Liquidate Long Aug 1 | Profit/ Loss |
		Price	Date	Loss			
1970	24.25				23.55		+70
1971	21.25				20.40		+85
1972	29.22				28.60		+62
1973	42.00	43.00	July 3	-100		58.62	+3124
1974	36.82	37.82	July 8	-100		38.45	+126
1975	51.22	52.22	July 7	-100		57.77	+1110
1976	47.15				42.35		+480

100% CORRECT IN 7 YEARS
50.57 POINTS PROFIT
3.00 POINTS LOSS
$14,271 NET PROFIT

Rules:
1. Sell short August hogs on the first trading day in July.
2. Use a 100-point stop above the closing.
3. If the stop is hit, reverse the position to a long position being long twice the amount you shorted.
4. Liquidate the long position August 1.
5. Liquidate the short position August 15.

Let's walk through a trade to see how the trade works. Taking 1974 as an example, the closing price on July 1 was 36.82 which means we would sell short with a stop 100 points above 36.82 at 37.82. Prices reached 37.82 the eighth day in July where we took our 100 point loss and bought long two contracts. We liquidated the long position on August 1 at 38.45 for a net profit of 126 points (63 points profit multiplied by two contracts). Since we had two contracts and the total profit was 126 points, we had a net gain for the year of .26 for this particular trade. Note that despite the fact 1974 showed a small profit, 1975 showed a substantial profit as did 1973 and the rest of the years.

Frequently in board rooms, you will hear traders or brokers saying that hogs follow bellies. This may be true, but if you walk outside the brokerage house and go to another firm, you will hear these traders saying that bellies follow the hogs. This is like the argument about which came first, the chicken or the egg. The next time you hear it, you would be better off if you just realized that both hogs and bellies can work independently of each other. There does not seem to be an established tendency for one to follow the other. Just as one starts to apparently follow the other, you can rest assured that it will be reversed.

OATS

When it comes to the grain markets, without a doubt, oats are the most lackluster performer of the entire complex of soybeans, wheat and corn.

In terms of the number of bushels grown in this country, the oat crop is substantial; however, the cash value of the oat crop doesn't even compare to that of the more important grains. Oats are primarily used for animal feed and only some 15% of oats are used for breakfast foods and human consumption.

Usually oats are harvested in early August so most of the facts and figures are known sometime in the October-November period.

Most seasonal work done in oats has been spreading oats and corn due to the fact corn is also used as a feed grain. However, our study shows that this does not appear to be a particularly valid way of trading the market.

We have isolated four extremely good oat trades that we would like to present to you now.

OAT TRADE #1

Since 1960, this trade has been correct in all years except 1974 and 1975, meaning it has been correct some 88% of the time. The interesting factor to note here is that we have been able to get data back to 1960. There has been a gain of 93.5 cents, a loss of 10.4 cents for a total gain of $4,155.

It should be noted that the win-loss ratio is very good here and the wins were eight times greater than the losses.

We also want to point out that the results from 1960, 1961 and 1962 were "eyeballed" from the chart. What we are showing on the following tabulation is the percent of profit and losses each year since 1960.

Trade Rules:

Buy long December oats on the first trading day in December. Liquidate on the next to the last day the December contract trades. Use a three-cent stop or four percent of the market value on December 1, whichever is greater.

OAT TRADE #1

	Profit/ Loss
1960	+4.5
1961	+4.0
1962	+4.0
1963	+3.0
1964	+9.0
1965	+6.0
1966	+1.0
1967	+7.0
1968	+1.0
1969	+3.0
1970	+2.0
1971	+2.0
1972	+20.0
1973	+15.0
1974	-4.0
1975	-6.4
1976	+12.0

* Results are eyeballed from chart.

88% CORRECT SINCE 1960
93.5 POINTS PROFIT
10.4 POINTS LOSS
$4,155 NET PROFIT

Rules:
1. Buy long December Oats on the first trading day in December.
2. Use a 3¢ stop or 4% of the market value on December 1, whichever is greater.
3. Liquidate on the next to the last day the December contract trades.

OAT TRADE #2

This trade attempts to capitalize on the tendency for oat prices to rally during the summer months. The trade has produced 95.8 cents of profit and 7.6 cents of losses. It has been correct 57% of the time for a net gain of 88.2 cents or $4,410.

Trade Rules:

Buy long one contract of July oats on the close of business May 6. If prices are lower by one cent on May 15, liquidate. Take a 20 point profit automatically on the long position. Liquidate the long or short position on June 15. It should be pointed out that if you sell on May 15 because prices are one cent lower, you would not reverse the trade, you just accept the loss you have at that point.

The most notable aspect of this trade is that it has produced some dynamite gains of 20 points per year each of the last four years. Prior to the 1973 market, the trade was good but not as spectacular as the profits seen in the 1973, 1974, 1975 and 1976 time period.

OAT TRADE #2

	Buy Long May 6	May 15	20¢ TARGET Date	Price	June 15	Profit/ Loss
1963	66.8	67.6			68.1	+1.3
1964	63.6	62.7 (Out)				-.9
1965	71.1	69.7 (Out)				-1.4
1966	67.5	68.7			69.0	+1.5
1967	71.3	71.1			70.0	-1.3
1968	69.3	67.6 (Out)				-1.7
1969	66.1	64.2 (Out)				-1.9
1970	63.2	64.8			66.7	+3.5
1971	67.3	67.6			76.8	+9.5
1972	69.1	69.0			68.7	-.4
1973	94.0	94.5	June 5	114.0		+20.0
1974	118.7	134.7	June 7	138.7		+20.0
1975	144.2	151.5	May 22	164.2		+20.0
1976	150.7	158.0	May 27	170.7		+20.0

Rules:
1. Buy long July Oats on the close of business May 6.
2. If prices are lower by 1¢ on May 15, liquidate.
3. Take a 20-point profit.
4. Liquidate long position on June 15.

OAT TRADE #3

This trade works on the fact that oats usually decline in value during the latter part of the summer months. The trade recap shows that it has produced 126.7 cents of profit, 22.4 cents of loss for a net gain of 104.3 and a dollar gain of $5,215. The trade has been correct 82% of the time.

Trade Rules:

Sell short one contract of December oats on July 1. Liquidate the position, taking a profit on August 1. Use a stop of 5% of the value of the closing price on July 1. If the stop is hit, reverse the position and buy long. Liquidate the long position on August 15. Liquidate the short position on August 1.

As an example, in 1973 the closing price on July 1 was 105.0; however, the five percent stop factor of 5.2 cents would have stopped us out on July 17 at 110.2. Prices on August 15 were 149.5 for a net gain of 39.3 cents for the trade, minus the 5.2 cent loss taken earlier on the trade, means there would have been a net profit of 34.1 points.

OAT TRADE #3

	July 1	5% STOP Price	Date	Loss	Aug 1	Aug 15	Profit/ Loss
1961	75.2				73.0		+2.2
1962	70.5				65.7		+4.8
1963	73.5				66.6		+6.9

| | July 1 | 5% STOP | | | Aug 1 | Aug 15 | Profit/ |
		Price	Date	Loss			Loss
1964	65.7				65.6		+ .1
1965	70.1				69.1		+1.0
1966	77.3				75.6		+1.7
1967	70.6				71.0		-.4
1968	66.0				61.6		+4.4
1969	65.0				62.2		+2.8
1970	67.5				68.2		- .7
1971	74.1				65.2		+8.9
1972	73.2				74.7		-1.5
1973	105.0	110.2	July 17	-5.2		149.5	+39.3
1974	154.5	162.2	July 15	-7.7		176.7	+14.5
1975	138.0	144.9	July 18	-6.9		171.0	+26.1
1976	185.0				171.0		+14.0

82% CORRECT IN 15 YEARS
126.7 POINTS PROFIT
22.4 POINTS LOSS
$5,215 NET PROFIT

Rules:
1. Sell short December Oats on July 1.
2. Use a stop that is equal to 5% of the value of the closing price on July 1.
3. If stop is hit, reverse the position and be long 1 contract.
4. Liquidate short position August 1.
5. Liquidate long position on August 15.

The key to this trade, obviously, is that if prices move against you, you must liquidate and instead of getting out of the long position on August 1, you get out of the long position on August 15. The underlying characteristic of this trade is that prices decline from July to August. This has been correct 57% of the time, so on that basis, the tendency is somewhat marginal; however, we have been able to compensate for this with a reversal factor. The reversal factor of all the seasonal tendency trades is extremely important, simply because when what should happen doesn't happen, you can rest assured that the market is usually going to have a substantial move in the new direction.

This trade is with the May oats and takes advantage of the fact prices decline from mid-January into April. The trade has produced a $5,065 profit since 1960. That is some 17 years of trading with only a loss of $175. It has been correct 94% of the time. Considering the large time span under study here—17 years—we feel this is one of the bread and butter seasonal tendency trades.

Trade Rules:

Sell short one contract of May oats on January 15. Liquidate on April 1 taking your profit or loss.

Those are the only rules needed for this trade and the only loss occurred in 1968 when one would have sold at 74.2 on January 15 and liquidated on April 1 at 77.7 for a net loss of 3.5 points. What is remarkable here is that we have only one loss of a meager $175 in the entire 17-year time span. This is highly significant.

OAT TRADE #4

	Jan 15	Apr 1	Profit/ Loss
1960	74.7	74.5	+.2
1961	66.5	60.2	+6.3
1962	73.2	70.1	+3.1
1963	70.1	69.2	+.9
1964	77.0	64.1	+12.9
1965	71.2	70.2	+1.0
1966	71.8	68.6	+3.2
1967	75.6	73.5	+2.1
1968	74.2	77.7	-3.5
1969	71.0	67.3	+3.7
1970	67.1	64.2	+2.9
1971	79.5	70.5	+9.0
1972	73.7	69.1	+4.6
1973	91.5	84.5	+7.0
1974	158.1	121.0	+37.1
1975	163.5	157.2	+6.3
1976	152.7	148.2	+4.5

Rules:
1. Sell short May Oats on January 15.
2. Liquidate on April 1.

ORANGE JUICE

Throughout the years, orange juice traders have referred to many seasonal patterns in orange juice. One of the most frequent patterns is for the price of orange juice to start a rally during the second week in October. However, we were not able to put together a profitable seasonal tendency trade that would work year in and year out.

What we did find was one trade, and only one trade, that has a long string of direct hits in the orange juice market.

ORANGE JUICE TRADE #1

The trade produced 3,765 points of profit, 565 points of loss for a net 32.00 cents or $4,800. It has been correct eight years and incorrect two years for an 80% accuracy rate.

Trade Rules:

Sell short March orange juice on December 15. Take profits on January 15. Use a stop protection of .5 cents or close out the position if there is a loss as of January 1.

ORANGE JUICE TRADE #1

	Sell Short Dec 15	5¢ Stop	Liquidate Jan 1	Liquidate Jan 15	Profit/ Loss
1967	65.40			57.30	+810
1968	48.75	53.75			-500
1969	45.25		45.90		-65
1970	37.70			33.80	+390

	Sell Short Dec 15	5¢ Stop	Liquidate Jan 1	Liquidate Jan 15	Profit/ Loss
1971	61.70			59.40	+230
1972	49.75			44.40	+535
1973	58.75			53.20	+555
1974	55.80			49.05	+675
1975	60.60			59.05	+155
1976	43.55			39.40	+415

80% CORRECT IN 10 YEARS
3,765 POINTS PROFIT
565 POINTS LOSS
$4,800 NET PROFIT

Rules:
1. Sell short March Orange Juice on December 15.
2. Use a stop of 5 cents or close out position if there is a loss as of January 1.
3. Take profits January 15.

PLYWOOD

Like potatoes, we found only one seasonal tendency with an extreme degree of reliability in the plywood market. However, this trade and tendency is one of the strongest in the book. If you study the price of plywood and lumber, you will quickly notice that there has always been a rally in the latter part of the year and the first part of the new year. There are some fundamental reasons for this — basically due to retailers of plywood lumber yards, etc., stocking up on the commodity for the spring and summer boom in building and housing starts.

PLYWOOD TRADE # 1

The trade has been right 100% of the time since 1971, which is as far back as we have data for this particular trade. The trade has shown a net profit of 14,160 points or net gain of $9,785.

The fact that we are not devoting much space in the book to this particular trade should not cause you to pass over this trade. Without a doubt, this is one of the strongest seasonal tendencies in the entire market. All you have to do to prove this is to study the price of plywood, and you will see how successful this tendency has been. Interestingly enough, very few people, even within the industry, are aware of this strong seasonal tendency. Frequently we have talked to those who own lumber yards who are not aware of the trade and, in fact, are selling plywood and lumber short during the winter months because they are expecting prices to decline prior to the summer boom in housing starts. If only they would have taken time to study the markets, they would have discovered, to their profit, the true seasonal tendency of this market.

Though we have not tested the same trade rules on lumber, we suspect the rules would be similiarly applicable.

Trade Rules:

You buy long the May contract on December 1. You sell and take your profit on the 8th day in March each year. Though a stop had never been needed for the trade, we suggest that one use the stop that would be a closing price one tick below the November lows.

PLYWOOD TRADE #1

	Price on Dec 1	Price on Mar 8	Profit
1971	79.20	107.70	28.50
1972	91.30	101.60	10.30
1973	136.00	167.40	31.40
1974	98.50	138.00	39.50
1975	110.50	127.40	16.90
1976	139.50	154.50	15.00

100% CORRECT SINCE 1971
141.60 POINTS PROFIT
0 LOSS
$9,785 NET PROFIT

Rules:
1. Buy long May Plywood on December 1.
2. Use a stop that is one tick lower than the lowest November close.
3. Take a profit on March 8.

PORK BELLIES

In fine cars there is the Rolls Royce, in fine wines there is Gran Cruz. In commodity trading there are soybeans and pork bellies. *Without a doubt* pork bellies are one of the most active and most exciting commodities. It is a humdinger providing the trader and investor alike with ample opportunities for gains. . .or losses!

Just in case you didn't know, there are actually two "bellies" to each hog. These bellies are cut off in slabs and are then frozen in storage until sliced for bacon. Obviously, there is only one way you can get a pork belly and that's from a hog. So the fundamentalists watch all sorts of wierd figures relating to hogs and feed; hogs to cattle; even the sex life, assuming he has one, with farrowing intentions. About 10% of each hog's weight ends up in bacon.

We have found several great seasonal trades here--several that have produced profits every year. Before revealing these, we'd like to give you some general seasonal patterns we noticed in our research.

There is a strong tendency for the February contract to go off the board weak. Thus a nimble trader would be prepared to take any sell signal four to five weeks before the contract expires around the 20th of January. Another strong tendency is for the July contract to stage a vigorous rally on or about March 1. There have been several seasonal tops of major importance around September 11 to 15.

PORK BELLY TRADE #1

Let's start the year off right with our first belly trade, one that tells us to buy long the August contract on the first trading day of the year. Yes, you could buy the February contract, but we have not been able to get data for the February basis as far back as for August, so August is used here.

Trade Rules:

Buy long the first trading day of the year with a buy stop at the closing price of the last day of the old year. For example, if prices closed at 36.50 the last day of the old year, you would place a buy stop order at that price with your broker.

If prices rally 400 points before January 16, grab your profit and tell someone else about this amazing book. After January 16, accept a profit equal to 4% of your entry price. Liquidate the position on the close of January 16 if prices are above the 4% target. For example, the 1968 entry price was 31.90 cents. Multiply 31.90 by 4% and you will get 1.27 cents. Add 1.27 cents back into 31.90 and we will have the 4% target at 33.17.

PORK BELLY TRADE #1

	Price	Date	4% Target	Date	Profit
1963	27.00	Jan 3	28.08	Jan 9	+1.08
1964	27.15	Jan 2	28.23	Jan 22	+1.08
1965	31.00	Jan 4	32.24	Jan 14	+1.24
1966	42.62	Jan 3	46.80	Jan 5	+4.18
1967	34.75	Jan 2	36.14	Jan 18	+1.39
1968	31.90	Jan 2	33.17	Feb 2	+1.27
1969	31.70	Jan 2	32.96	Jan 21	+1.26
1970	41.45	Jan 5	43.10	Feb 13	+1.65
1971	26.55	Jan 4	27.61	Feb 2	+1.06
1972	35.95	Jan 3	39.40	Jan 17	+3.45
1973	44.17	Jan 2	45.93	Jan 16	+1.76
1974	60.45	Jan 2	64.45	Jan 4	+4.00
1975	62.80	Jan 2	65.31	Jan 28	+2.51
1976	68.75	Jan 2	72.75	Jan 6	+4.00
1977	55.10	Jan 3	57.30	Feb 7	+2.20

100% CORRECT IN 14 YEARS
3213 POINTS PROFIT
$11,567 NET PROFIT

Rules:
1. Buy long August bellies the 1st trading of the year with a buy stop order that is the closing price of the last day of the year.
2. Take profits if prices rally 400 points.
3. After January 16, accept a profit equal to 4% of your entry price.
4. Sell on the close of January 16 if prices are above the 4% target.

In 14 years of trading, this trade has never failed. It has always worked. There was a total gain of 32.13 cents or $11,567 before commissions. Certainly this is not a trade to take lightly. What a nice way to start off the year! Also, realize that the 4% gain means we are usually making 50% gain on the margin required for this trade that has been correct 100% of the time.

PORK BELLY TRADE #2

In this next seasonal tendency trade, the trade has been wrong only once in the last fourteen years. The trade has produced 56.55 cents profit and 11.25 cents loss for a net dollar profit of $16,308. The one problem is that we had to reverse 35% of the time. Nonetheless, the reversing improved the total performance.

Trade Rules:

This trade in bellies is to sell short the July contract on April 12 or the nearest market day. However, if the market is closed on April 12, sell short on April 11. Do not sell short until prices close lower than the previous day. If April 11 or April 12 is an up-day, wait for the first down day, then sell short. The target for the trade is five percent of the entry price. Use a buy stop of five percent above your entry price so the position will be reversed to be long twice the amount of the short position.

PORK BELLY TRADE #2

	SELL SHORT		5% TARGET		5% REVERSE			Liquidate June 1	Profit/ Loss
	Date	Price	Date	Price	Date	Price	Loss		
1963	Apr 15	25.60	Apr 17	24.32					+1.28
1964	Apr 13	28.52	May 15	27.10					+1.42
1965	Apr 13	31.15			May 6	32.70	-155	36.35	+7.30
1966	Apr 12	44.50	May 19	42.28					+2.22
1967	Apr 12	34.75			May 5	36.48	-173	44.40	+15.84
1968	Apr 12	38.80	May 6	36.86					+1.94
1969	Apr 11	35.95			May 13	37.74	-179	40.70	+5.92
1970	Apr 14	42.90	May 15	40.76					+2.14
1971	Apr 12	27.25	Apr 21	25.89					+1.36

SELL SHORT		5% TARGET		5% REVERSE			Liquidate June 1	Profit/ Loss
Date	Price	Date	Price	Date	Price	Loss		
1972 Apr 12	41.67	Apr 24	39.59					+2.08
1973 Apr 12	52.67			May 11	55.30	-263	57.95	+5.30
1974 Apr 15	52.12	Apr 19	49.62					+2.50
1975 Apr 14	71.15			Apr 27	74.70	-355	76.40	+3.40
1976 Apr 13	77.15	May 11	73.30					+3.85

93% CORRECT IN 14 YEARS
5,655 POINTS PROFIT
1,125 POINTS LOSS
$16,308 NET PROFIT

Rules:
1. Sell short July bellies on April 12 or the nearest market day. However, if the market is closed on April 12, sell short on April 11. Do not sell short until prices close lower than the previous day. If April 11 or April 12 is an up-day, wait for the first down day, then sell short.
2. Use a sell stop 5% above your entry price so you will reverse and be net short twice the amount you were long in the event the trade fails.
3. The target is 5% of the entry price.

PORK BELLY TRADE #3

Moving right along, we come to the merry month of August where a splendid buying opportunity has been presented 85% of the time in the last twelve years. The total profits were $6,400; total points profit, 2178 and total points loss, 400.

Trade Rules:

The trade rules are simple. Buy long February bellies on the close of August 10. If the market is closed on August 10, buy long on the next market day. Place a straight stop of 200 points below where you are filled for the long. The target is five percent of the entry price

PORK BELLY TRADE #3

	Buy Long	200 POINT STOP		5% TARGET		Profit/ Loss
		Price	Date	Price	Date	
1965	34.72			36.45	Aug 16	+173
1966	36.07			37.87	Aug 16	+180
1967	33.20	31.20	Aug 29			-200
1968	29.85			31.34	Aug 15	+149
1969	37.30			39.16	Aug 27	+186
1970	30.77			32.30	Aug 17	+153
1971	28.17			29.57	Sept 14	+140
1972	42.15			44.25	Aug 28	+210
1973	80.40	78.40	Aug 17			-200
1974	56.20			59.01	Aug 14	+281
1975	86.10			90.40	Sept 5	+430
1976	55.35			58.11	Aug 18	+276

85% CORRECT IN 12 YEARS
2178 POINTS PROFIT
400 POINTS LOSS
$6,400 NET PROFIT

Rules:
1. Buy long February bellies on close of August 10. If market is closed, buy long the next day.
2. Target is 5% of entry price.
3. Use a straight stop of 200 points.

PORK BELLY TRADE #4

There has been an incredibly strong tendency for bellies to stage a market rally in early November. However, the few people that have written about this seasonal pattern have not been able to discover the rules that make it profitable. Here are ours--the rules that would have produced a profit 76% of the time with a net profit of some $10,753. The total number of profitable trades equalled some 37.33 cents while losing trades accounted for 7.46 cents. The net was 29.87 cents which again drives home the tremendous impact that seasonal tendencies do exert on the market.

Trade Rules:

The rules are simple. Buy long July bellies any day starting and including November 1 that prices trade above the highest price of the past four days. If prices move five percent below your entry price, accept the loss and wait for the next trade. Take profits of ten percent greater than your entry price.

If you buy long, your target can be established in one of three ways: (1) five percent of your entry price; (2) a straight 500 points; and, (3) the difference from the June low to the June high added to the high of June.

As an example in 1967, we sold short at 36.00 which meant we would take a profit of 3.60 cents at 32.40 where our target was established.

PORK BELLY TRADE #4

		BUY LONG	10% TARGET		5% STOP		Profit/
	Date	Price	Date	Price	Date	Price	Loss
1964	Dec 9	25.35	Jan 10	27.88			+2.53
1965	Nov 2	29.05	Jan 5	31.95			+2.90
1966	Nov 2	41.00	Nov 30	45.10			+4.10
1967	Nov 11	34.42	Dec 11	37.86			+3.44
1968	Nov 7	32.85	Mar 28	36.13			+3.28
1969	Nov 13	31.80	Feb 17	34.98			+3.18
1970	Nov 3	41.35	Jan 30	45.48			+4.13
1971	Nov 4	32.07			Jan 15	30.31	-1.76
1972	Nov 9	31.40	Dec 16	34.54			+3.14
1973	Nov 1	43.97	Jan 8	48.36			+4.39
1974	Nov 1	63.80			Dec 4	60.61	-3.19
1975	Nov 20	62.40	Nov 29	68.64			+6.24
1976	Nov 5	50.30			Nov 29	47.79	-2.51

76% CORRECT IN 13 YEARS
3733 POINTS PROFIT
746 POINTS LOSS
$10,753 NET PROFIT

Rules:

1. Buy long July bellies any day starting, and including November 1 that prices trade above the highest price of the previous 4 days.
2. Use a 5% stop.
3. Use a 10% target.

This particular trade with bellies is based on a penetration of the June highs. There has been a strong tendency for prices to rally in the July-August time period. However, to determine that we are going to see such a rally, we have found that if the trader uses the high point in June as a penetration level and it is exceeded, a very nice seasonal tendency trade can be established.

Since 1965 the trade has had one loss in twelve years, meaning it has been correct 92% of the time. The net profit during this time period was 66.37 cents or some $25,063. The only loss was for 3.25 cents or $1,170.

Trade Rules:

Determine the high and low for the month of June in the February pork belly contract. Buy long if the June high is penetrated. Sell short if the June low is penetrated.

If you buy long, your target can be established in one of three ways: 1, five percent of your entry price; 2, 500 points; or 3, the difference from the June low to the June high added to the high of June.

To explain the third alternative, let's look at 1973 as an example. The June high was 63.55 and the low was 53.00. If you take the difference in those two prices (10.55) and add that to 63.55, a target of 74.10 is determined.

For the long position, use a stop that is the June low or 500 points, whichever is the greater.

If you sell short, use a target that is ten percent of the entry price. Use a stop that is 500 points or the June high whichever occurs first.

As an example, in 1967, we sold short at 36.00 which meant we would take a profit of 3.60 cents at 32.40 where our target was established.

The stop is five cents or the June high whichever occurs first.

In observing this trade, you will notice that despite the rather complicated trade rules, it has not been subject to severe whipsaws. Nonetheless this is the type of seasonal trade that is probably best left to the experienced trader--the one who is going to follow the market on a closer basis.

PORK BELLY TRADE #5

	June High	June Low	Taken Date	Date	Date	Price	Profit/ Loss
1965	36.15	30.10		July 1	Nov 15	42.20	+6.05
1966	31.50	29.47		July 5	Aug 8	36.50	+5.00
1967	39.52	36.00		July 10	Aug 31	32.40	+3.60
1968	34.35	31.10		July 1	July 19	31.10	-3.25
1969	37.80	34.00		July 9	Sept 23	42.80	+5.00
1970	34.77	30.30		Aug 11	Dec 28	25.53	+4.77
1971	35.80	31.30		July 6	Aug 18	27.17	+4.13
1972	43.55	37.55		July 18	Nov 28	48.55	+5.00
1973	63.55	53.00		July 2	July 23	74.10	+10.55
1974	47.47	36.30		July 1	July 24	58.64	+11.17
1975	78.50	70.32		July 2	Aug 26	86.68	+8.18
1976	71.20	61.70		July 14	Aug 2	55.53	+6.17

92% CORRECT IN 12 YEARS
6,952 POINTS PROFIT
325 POINTS LOSS
$25,063 NET PROFIT

Rules:
1. Determine the high and low for February bellies for the month of June.
2. Buy long if the June high is penetrated. If you buy long, establish a target in one of three ways whichever is the greatest:
   a. 5% of the entry price
   b. 500 points
   c. The difference from the June low to the June high added to the high of June. Use a stop that is the June low or 500 points, whichever is greater.
3. Sell short if the June low is penetrated. The target is 10% of the entry price. Use a stop that is 500 points or the June high whichever occurs first.

PORK BELLY TRADE #6

This trade attempts to capitalize on the apparent decline of belly prices from April into May and sometimes June or July. The trade rules are very simple. However, it should be pointed out that in the last 14 years, the trade has been wrong six times. This is not a high batting average in terms of percentage correct; however, the profits are statistically significant.

The dollar gain here is substantial—some $20,300 over the 14-year time period. If you study your charts, you will see there is a stronger tendency for prices to decline than the trade rules might illustrate at first glance.

Trade Rules:

Sell short the August pork belly contract on April 18. The target is 10% of the entry price. If prices move 5% against your position, close out the position.

It should be noted that additional rules could be made which would make this trade more accurate in terms of right and wrong percentage. These rules would be that if you reversed and doubled up on the 5% stop, instead of just being stopped out, you would take profits on July 1 and you would have had an extremely profitable trade on the long side.

Had you done that, you would have a gain of 77.53 cents; a loss of 21.14 cents with a total gain of 56.39 cents or $20,300. It would have been profitable to do this reversing on the 5% stop in all years but 1969. So traders should watch this in the event that you decide to take this seasonal tendency for additional protection.

PORK BELLY TRADE #6

	Sell Short April 18	5% STOP			Liquidate Reversal On July 1	10% TARGET		
		Price	Date	Loss		Price	Date	
1963	24.75	25.98	May 13	-1.23	29.45			+6.94
1964	29.10					26.19	May 27	+2.91
1965	32.30	33.91	May 10	-1.61	41.20			+14.58
1966	43.80					39.42	May 18	+4.38
1967	34.55	36.27	May 5	-1.72	39.00			+5.46
1968	39.00					35.10	May 7	+3.90
1969	35.50	37.27	Apr 29	-1.77	32.95			-8.64
1970	40.60					36.54	May 26	+4.06
1971	25.75					23.18	June 29	+2.57
1972	40.50					36.45	May 19	+4.05
1973	52.27	54.88	May 14	-2.61	59.65			+9.54
1974	50.40					45.31	Apr 26	+5.09
1975	71.25	74.81	Apr 25	-3.56	78.00			+6.38
1976	76.72					69.05	May 17	+7.67

Rules:
1. Seli short August bellies on April 18.
2. Use a 5% stop.
3. Use a 10% target.

(Optional rules)
4. If stop is hit, reverse and buy long doubling the position.
5. Take a 5% target.

A good friend of ours says that bellies are like the National Football League—on any given day, either team can win! And so it is with bellies which are frequently up and down the day's limit during one day's trading session. The volatility of this market makes them an ideal trading selection.

POTATOES

In the last four years, we have seen two definite attempts to manipulate the potato market by large traders and/or potato processors. This has been one of the many drawbacks to this market in our view. The potato market tends to be one of the most volatile markets of them all. It is somewhat similar to the egg market in that prices are extremely erratic. Why does this happen? We suspect that because the margin requirements on potatoes tend to be extremely low, the type of speculator drawn to this market is one who has little money. Our experience in the market tells us one thing for certain--people with small amounts of money in the market tend to be: one, less knowledgeable about the market than those with large amounts of money; and two, much more emotional. This emotional factor, we believe, is what causes such erratic activity in the potato market.

There are two types of potato contracts. One is the Maine potato and the other is the Idaho potato. The Idaho potato contract has been trading only since 1968 and that is a little sketchy in this particular contract. As with all commodities, there are some seasonal factors influencing prices—weather conditions, planting conditions, rainfall, etc. There is a winter crop, an early spring crop, a late spring crop and an early summer crop of potatoes. The early crops account for about 20% of the U.S. total output of potatoes and are harvested sometime in the spring of the year no later than June 30.

We could only find one potato trade which satisfied all of the criteria we had established for a seasonal tendency trade to be listed in this book.

POTATO TRADE #1

This particular trade has been correct 93% of the time and has produced a total profit of 450 points and a total loss of 30 points with a net gain of 420 points. Since each point is worth $5, there is a total gain of $2,100.

Trade Rules:

The trade rules are easy. Notice the high of the May potato contract in October. Once the October high is penetrated, purchase long. Automatically take a 50 point profit. Use a stop-loss of 30 points.

POTATO TRADE #1

	October High	Entry Date	50-Point Profit	Date Exit Position	Profit/ Loss
1963	2.68	Dec 26	3.18	Mar 23	+50
1964	4.93	Nov 24	5.43	Nov 30	+50
1965	3.60	Mar 4	4.10	Mar 16	+50
1966	4.20	Nov 22	4.70	Dec 28	+50
1967	3.94	NO TRADE			
1968	3.83	Nov 11	3.53	Dec 13	-30
1969	3.56	Nov 3	4.06	Dec 22	+50
1970	3.99	NO TRADE			
1971	3.74	Nov 23	4.24	Feb 1	+50
1972	5.65	Nov 10	6.15	Dec 12	+50
1973	8.92	Nov 13	9.42	Nov 19	+50
1974	7.48	NO TRADE			
1975	19.15	NO TRADE			
1976	8.30	Nov 12	8.80	Nov 15	+50

93% CORRECT IN 14 YEARS
450 POINTS PROFIT
30 POINTS LOSS
$2,100 NET PROFIT

Rules:
1. If the October high of May potatoes is penetrated, buy long.
2. Use a 30-point stop loss.
3. Take a 50-point profit.

Notice that there were years when this trade was not applicable. Specifically, the trade was not operative in 1967, 1970 as well as 1974. The remainder of the time the trade should have been put on and the theoretical profits are quite good considering the trade has been wrong only once in 14 years of study.

There are other seasonal aspects in the potato market and we have seen other people produce seasonal trades in the market. However, a closer observation has taught us to be somewhat wary of other seasonal trades in this market. Obviously, we would like to present the reader with more than one potato trade, but that's all we could find having an assurance of being repetitive. Therefore, that's all we can give you.

Observation:

We did notice spud prices usually rally in March and decline in July, August and September.

SOYBEANS

Perhaps it's due to our enjoyment in trading the soybean market that we have come up with more seasonal tendencies for soybeans than any other commodity. We have eight seasonal trades for this particular market.

Soybeans are without a doubt the king of all future contracts currently being traded. They tend to be more volatile, have larger daily ranges and are widely enough traded to allow relatively easy entrance and exits for the trader. There is some good fundamental information that helps the soybean trader, primarily the government release of the Planting Intentions in March which tells what the intentions of the farmers are for planting acreage in soybeans. Thus, one can tell approximately how large the crops should be. Then, in early July, a crop reduction report is also issued which tells what the planted acreage estimates are.

Ultimately the price of soybeans depend on the price of the soybean oil and soybean meal made from the beans minus whatever it costs to process the beans and distribute these items. Therefore the ultimate price of soybeans will be determined by the availability of oils and meal or meal substitutes throughout the world. The soybean crop tends to be harvested in late September and may run all the way to November. Once the November time period has been reached and the entire crop has been harvested, that's it. No more beans will be available until the following crop. Incidently, the advent of WW II is when the U.S. got into the soybean business; we are now the largest soybean exporter.

The strongest seasonal tendency in soybean prices is seen by the price rise starting sometime during January and carrying through into April.

SOYBEAN TRADE #1

This trade has been wrong three times during the last 14 years, which means its accuracy level is 79%. It has a net gain of 186.2 cents, a net loss of 21.8 cents, for a total profit of 164.4 cents, and a dollar gain of $8,220. This is good.

Trade Rules:

The trade rules are simple. Buy the May contract of soybeans on the close of the first trading day in January. Place a stop ten points below your entry price. Take your profits or loss January 31 or the last trading day in January.

As an example, in 1966 the closing price on January 2 was 276.0. The stop would have been 266.0. Prices never declined that low. The lowest point to which prices declined was 270.5 and the trade was liquidated on January 31 at 287.0 for a net gain of 11.0 cents.

The largest loss one could suffer in the trade would be ten cents, and that occurred only in 1975 and 1964. The other loss was in 1967 for a meager 1.8 cents. Gains have run all the way from 1.5 cents up to 51.0 cents. The accuracy of this trade in terms of the win-loss ratio, as well as the percentage of times correct, should place it high on the trader's list of seasonal tendency trades.

SOYBEAN TRADE #1

	Buy Long	10 POINT STOP		Liquidate	Profit/ Loss
		Price	Date		
1963	252.1			270.7	+18.6
1964	285.2	275.2	Jan 22		-10.0
1965	282.7			309.7	+27.0
1966	276.0			287.1	+11.1
1967	290.1			288.3	-1.8
1968	274.3			277.6	+3.3
1969	265.8			267.1	+1.3
1970	254.8			258.2	+3.4
1971	302.5			311.1	+8.6
1972	316.5			319.3	+2.8

| | Buy Long | 10 POINT STOP | | Liquidate | Profit/ Loss |
		Price	Date		
1973	416.5			467.5	+51.0
1974	600.7			649.5	+48.8
1975	737.5	727.5	Jan 3		-10.0
1976	465.7			476.0	+10.3

79% CORRECT IN 14 YEARS
1,862 POINTS PROFIT
218 POINTS LOSS
$8,220 NET PROFIT

Rules:
1. Buy long May beans on the close of the first trading day in January.
2. Use a stop 10 points below your entry price.
3. Liquidate position January 31 or the last trading day in January.

SOYBEAN TRADE #2

This trade has been correct 90% of the time, which means it has been wrong only once in the last eleven years. It has a gain of 192.5 points and a loss of 26.4 cents for a total gain of 166.1 cents and a dollar gain of $8,305.

Trade Rules:

Rules for this trade are somewhat more complicated than the previous one. Find the low price for November beans during the month of December. Buy long on January 4 if prices are above that low. Reverse, selling short twice the amount you were long if prices fall below the December low. Take profits on April 15 for the long position. If the position is reversed to the short side, the target is the same amount as your loss. For example, in 1969 the buy price was 242.6 and the stop was 239.2. The stop was hit giving a loss of 3.4 and, at that time, the position would have been reversed. On the short side, the target, with twice the number of contracts, would be the amount of the loss or 3.4 cents. If the target on the short side has not been hit by April 2, cover the position on the close of April 2.

There are some years when you would have reversed from the long side to the short side; but our reversal rule has well accounted for the market activity and has shown profits on a rather consistent basis for this trade.

SOYBEAN TRADE #2

REVERSAL

	Dec Low	Jan 4	Price	Date	Loss	Target	Date Out	Liquidation Price	Apr 15	Net Profit/ Loss
1963	237.0	241.5							245.0	+3.5
1964	252.0	256.2	251.8	Mar 9	-4.4	247.4	Mar 20	247.4		+4.4
1965	248.0	249.7							257.7	+8.0
1966	251.3	260.0							278.8	+18.8
1967	280.0	272.0								No Trade
1968	269.2	268.7								No Trade
1969	239.2	242.6	239.2	Feb 17	-3.4	235.8	Mar 7	235.8		+3.4
1970	240.7	242.7							256.7	+14.0
1971	275.7	278.3							283.0	+4.7
1972	304.5	301.1								No Trade
1973	330.5	351.0							427.7	+76.7
1974	577.0	608.0	577.0	Mar 27	-31.0	546.0	Apr 2	546.0		+31.0
1975	661.0	689.0	661.0	Jan 8	-28.0	633.0	Jan 15	633.0		+28.0
1976	484.0	489.0	484.0	Jan 28	-5.0	479.0	Apr 1	494.7		-26.4

90% CORRECT IN 11 YEARS
19,250 POINTS PROFIT
264 POINTS LOSS
$8,305 NET GAIN

Rules:
1. Find the low for November beans during the month of December.
2. If prices are above that low on January 4, buy long.
3. Reverse position selling short twice the amount of the long position if prices fall below the December low.
4. Take profits on long position on April 15.
5. Target for short side is amount of loss on initial reversal. If target is not reached by April 2, liquidate.

This trade has been 77% correct with a gain of 912.6 cents, a loss of 29.4 cents for a net gain of 883.2 cents or $44,160. The net profit figure on this trade is extremely high, indicating to us that this is one of those trades that can really turn tiger, creating substantial and sizable profits for the seasonal trader.

Trade Rules:

Note the July bean price on January 2 and then again on April 1. If prices are higher on April 1, buy; if lower, sell short. Take profits July 1 on the long position. Take profits on the short position or liquidate the trade on June 15. The largest loss this trade saw was in 1971 when you would have sold at 300 and liquidated the short position at 324.8. There were some substantial gains—one of 418 cents in 1973, one of 93.5 cents in 1975 and one of 206 cents in 1976.

SOYBEAN TRADE #3

	January 2	April 1		June 15	July 1	Profit/ Loss
1963	253.0	258.7	(buy long)		275.0	+16.3
1964	286.7	257.5	(sell short)	247.8		+9.7
1965	281.0	305.7	(buy long)		296.0	-9.7
1966	276.8	288.6	(buy long)		368.0	+79.4
1967	289.7	286.1	(sell short)	286.3		-.2
1968	276.3	275.7	(sell short)	268.7		+7.0
1969	266.0	266.0	NO TRADE		NO TRADE	
1970	256.8	265.1	(buy long)		289.2	+24.1
1971	304.8	300.0	(sell short)	319.5		-19.5
1972	319.2	346.7	(buy long)		355.0	+8.3
1973	410.2	531.5	(buy long)		950.0	+418.5
1974	603.0	591.7	(sell short)	542.7		+49.0
1975	744.0	605.5	(sell short)	512.0		+93.5
1976	473.7	480.2	(buy long)		687.0	+206.8

77% CORRECT
9,126 POINTS PROFIT
2,940 POINTS LOSS
$44,160 NET PROFIT

Rules:
1. Note the July Bean price on January 2 and April 1.
2. If prices are higher on April 1, buy long.
3. If prices are lower on April 1, sell short.
4. Liquidate the long position on July 1.
5. Liquidate the short position on June 15.

SOYBEAN TRADE #4

This trade has been correct 11 out of the last 14 years meaning it has been right 79% of the time. This produced 161.5 cents of profit, 30 cents of loss for a net gain of 131.5 or $6,576.

Though this trade is not as spectacular as Soybean Trade #3, nonetheless it has a high degree of reliability and certainly is going to be one which traders want to follow.

Trade Rules:

Buy long the November soybean contract the next to the last day in September. Use a straight ten cent stop. Take profits on the long position November 15. If you are stopped out, buy back any time that prices close above your first entry price. Take profits on November 15 if you should again enter the position. If you get a 5% increase in value before November 15, take profits at that level.

SOYBEAN TRADE #4

	Buy Long	10¢ STOP		Liquidate 5% of Entry Price		Liquidate Nov 15	Profit/ Loss
		Price	Date	Price	Date		
1963	265.2					278.7	+13.5
1964	271.6					279.2	+7 6
1965	247.5					254.1	+6.6
1966	294.5					300.2	+5.7
1967	263.5					263.6	+.1
1968	249.6					256.3	+6.7
1969	284.2					306.1	+21.9

	Buy Long	10¢ STOP		Liquidate 5% of Entry Price		Liquidate Nov 15	Profit/ Loss
		Price	Date	Price	Date		
1970	236.8					246.2	+9.4
1971	310.5			326.0	Oct 15		+15.5
1972	344.7	334.7	Oct 9				-10.0
1973	630.0	620.0	Oct 1				-10.0
1974	838.0			882.0	Oct 1		+44.0
1975	564.0	554.0	Oct 2				-10.0
1976	621.5			652.0	Oct 5		+30.5

79% CORRECT IN 14 YEARS
161.5 POINTS PROFIT
30.0 POINTS LOSS
$6,576 NET PROFIT

Rules:
1. Buy long November beans on the next to the last day in September
2. Use a 10¢ stop.
3. If you are stopped out, buy back if prices close above your first entry price.
4. Take profits on November 15 or take profits if prices increase 5% of entry price.

SOYBEAN TRADE #5

This trade has been wrong only three times in the last 13 years, meaning it has been correct 77% of the time. The trade has produced 686.7 cents profit, 32.1 cents loss for a net gain of 654.6 cents or $32,730.

The trade capitalizes on the fact that the November soybean contract has tended to stage a rally during the summer months. However, it has been difficult to tell at what point one should get in for the possible summer rally in beans. Our trading rules, however, will handle this situation.

Trade Rules:

Determine what the high was for November beans during the month of March. Buy long when prices go above that level. If the contract is bought before July 1, sell on July 1. If the contract is bought after July 1, sell on November 15. Use a stop that is the low of the week when the long position is established.

There were some substantial gains, especially in 1973 and 1974; however, if we toss out the extraordinary years, including 1976, the trade is still on the profitable side with some substantial gains, even in the relatively inactive time period of 1963 through 1970. This is another one of those trades that soybean traders will want to follow closely.

SOYBEAN TRADE #5

	Bought Long March High	Date	STOPPED OUT		Liquidate July 1	Liquidate Nov 15	Profit/ Loss
			Price	Date			
1963	252.3	May 8			272.3		+20.0
1964	256.2	Aug 28				276.2	+20.0
1965	257.3	Apr 1	255.7	Apr 29			-1.6
1966	271.0	Apr 1			312.0		+41.0
1967	283.1	May 23	278.1	June 9			-5.0
1968	273.2	NO TRADE				NO TRADE	
1969	239.7	Sept 16				246.2	+6.5
1970	254.0	Apr 1			290.0		+36.0
1971	291.5	May 20			323.2		+31.7
1972	319.0	Apr 4			330.2		+11.2
1973	435.7	Apr 18			624.0		+188.3
1974	646.0	July 9				765.0	+119.0
1975	603.5	July 28	578.0	Aug 28			-25.5
1976	514.0	May 5			727.0		+213.0

77% CORRECT IN 13 YEARS
6,867 POINTS PROFIT
321 POINTS LOSS
$32,730 NET PROFIT

Rules:
1. Note the high for November beans in March.
2. Buy long when prices go above that March high.
3. Use a stop that is the low of the week when long position is established.
4. If position was established before July 1, liquidate on July 1.
5. If position is established after July 1, liquidate on November 15.

The trade recap on this trade is somewhat misleading given the market circumstance in 1973. There were 166.4 cents profit and loss of 73.9 cents for a total profit of 92.5 cents showing a net gain of $4,625. The trade was 64% correct. The one big loss occurred in 1973 with a loss of 66.0 cents. The other losses only totalled 7.9 cents or $395. Because of unusual trading circumstances in 1973, we can almost discount that year.

This trade is based on the ability of the market to rally from late June into early July.

Trade Rules:

Buy long November beans on June 26 and liquidate the position on July 5. Use a stop that is the low during the week you purchased.

We are showing this trade for two reasons: one, there has been a strong tendency for the trade to be correct with the exception of 1973; and secondly, just so you will keep in mind that years such as 1973 do occur. Things can change. Seasonal tendencies can be altered by radical markets; therefore, the intelligent trader is going to look for abnormal activity to see what effect it will have on seasonal traders. Personally, we feel that any soybean trader in the 1973 time period would have excluded most of the seasonal tendency trades. With the exception of 1973, the trade has a very good track record; however, again the admonition is that one must be careful. Time periods such as seen in that hectic market may occur again.

SOYBEAN TRADE #6

	Buy Long June 26	Stopped Out	Liquidate July 5	Profit/ Loss
1963	256.7		272.0	+15.3
1964	242.7		244.7	+2.0
1965	248.0	246.7		-1.3
1966	299.0		314.5	+15.5
1967	275.3	274.8		-.5
1968	255.3	255.1		-.2
1969	235.6		237.5	+1.9
1970	284.5		286.5	+2.0
1971	317.7		326.1	+8.4
1972	318.7		329.0	+10.3

	Buy Long June 26	Stopped Out	Liquidate July 5	Profit/ Loss
1973	654.0		588.0	-66.0
1974	568.2		616.2	+48.0
1975	504.7		498.8	-5.9
1976	684.2		747.2	+63.0

64% CORRECT IN 14 YEARS
1,664 POINTS PROFIT
739 POINTS LOSS
$4,625 NET PROFIT

Rules:
1. Buy long November beans on June 26.
2. Use a STOP that is the low during the week of purchase.
3. Liquidate July 5.

SOYBEAN TRADE #7

This trade is based on the tendency for soybean prices to rally from August into September and October.

This trade has been 93% correct which means there has been only one loss in the last 14 years of trading. It has produced 197.7 cents profit; 0.7 cents loss and a net gain of $9,850 profit. This trade is extremely good when we consider the risk-reward ratio was almost a miniscule loss compared to the gains that have rolled up year in and year out since 1963. Obviously, astute traders are going to want to follow this one closely.

Trade Rules:

Buy long November soybeans on August 10. Check the low of the week of September 10 and close out the position if that low is violated. Take a 25-point profit from the August 10 close. If you do not receive a 25-point profit by October 15, take a profit on the close of that day.

	Buy Long Aug 10	LOW OF 9/10		25-POINT TARGET		25-Point Profit	Date	Liquidate Oct 15	Profit/ Loss
		Price	Date	Price	Date				
1963	252.0	254.7		277.0	Sept 27				+25.0
1964	243.8	253.7		268.8	Sept 14				+25.0
1965	245.3	245.5	Sept 13						+.2
1966	317.2	316.5	Sept 13						-.7
1967	266.2	266.3	Sept. 22						-0-
1968	251.8	252.5	Sept 26						+.7
1969	236.6	234.8						244.7	+8.1
1970	280.2	280.5						297.2	+17.0
1971	318.5	319.1	Sept 3						+.6
1972	331.1	337.2	Sept 11						+6.1
1973	849.0	610.5				889.0	Aug 13		+40.0*
1974	794.0	731.0				819.0	Aug 19		+25.0
1975	602.7	556.0	Sept 11			627.7	Aug 18		+25.0
1976	629.0	735.0				654.0	Aug 19		+25.0

*Market opened limit up giving a 40.0 point profit.

93% CORRECT IN 14 YEARS
1,977 POINTS PROFIT
7 POINTS LOSS
$9,850 NET PROFIT

Rules:

1. Buy long November beans on August 10.
2. Check the low of the week of September 10 and close out the position if that low is violated.
3. Target should be 25 points from the close on August 10.
4. Liquidate on the close of October 15 if 25 point profit has not been taken.

SOYBEAN TRADE #8

This trade operates, again, on the tendency for prices to rally during the summer months. We have isolated a factor that tells us when this rally should occur during any given time period.

This trade has occurred eight times since 1962 and has been wrong once, which means it has been 88% correct. It has produced a gain of 487.4 cents, a loss of 2.3 cents for a net profit of 485.1 or a net dollar gain of $24,255.

Like trade #7, this trade is also extremely attractive considering the miniscule loss of only 2.3 cents which occurred in 1969. There have been some substantial gains; However, even if we kick out those gains which occurred in 1973 and 1976, the trade is still well ahead on the plus side.

Trade rules:

Determine the price of November beans on April 1. If they are above the April 1 level on May 15, buy long. Take your profits on the first trading day in July.

SOYBEAN TRADE #8

	April 1	May 15	Liquidate July 1	Profit/ Loss
1962	240.0	238.2		
1963	246.0	251.7	272.6	+20.9
1964	247.1	239.5		
1965	256.8	247.6		
1966	272.5	277.3	312.0	+34.7
1967	279.7	277.5		
1968	267.0	262.5		
1969	235.2	237.6	235.3	-2.3
1970	254.1	258.1	289.2	+31.1
1971	286.7	289.0	323.2	+34.2
1972	315.5	318.5	330.2	+11.7
1973	412.8	479.5	624.0	+144.5
1974	562.0	541.0		
1975	577.0	496.0		
1976	506.5	536.7	747.0	+210.3

88% CORRECT IN 8 YEARS
4,874 POINTS PROFIT
23 POINTS LOSS
$24,255 NET PROFIT

Rules:
1. Check price of November beans of April 1.
2. If prices are above the April 1 high on May 15, buy long.
3. Take profits on the first trading day in July.

MORE ABOUT BEANS. . .

The soybean stocks is a percentage usage figure and appears to be an extremely reliable indicator of long-term markets. When there is a low level of soybean stocks relative to usage, we are told that soybeans are in short supply and to expect substantially higher prices.

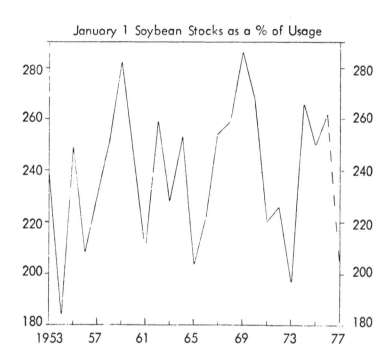

January 1 Soybean Stocks as a % of Usage

The way one arrives at this figure is to determine the soybean stocks compared to the usage to date. As you can see, when this figure was very low, such as in 1953, the early 1960's and again in 1965 and 1973, we saw substantial bull markets begin. This should be interesting because the current figure is again at the low level reading and would forecast higher soybean prices for 1977.

125

SOYBEAN MEAL

The third part of the soybean complex triad is soybean meal where we have isolated two reliable soybean meal trades.

SOYBEAN MEAL TRADE #1

This trade has been 100% correct since 1963. It has a net gain of 18,255 points or $18,255. Considering that the trade has been 100% correct during the last 14 years, this must go on the top of any seasonal trader's list of trades to study.

Trade Rules:

The trade rules are very simple. Buy long one contract of March meal on May 1. Take your profits on July 1. If by the time July 1 has rolled around, and you have a loss or are even, place a stop five percent below your entry price and liquidate, taking profits on August 15.

Though it was never needed, you should probably have a ten percent stop on the initial position entered into on May 1.

This trade has produced some outstanding results, especially in 1976 and 1973; and, it has consistently been profitable. Notice that it even took a substantial profit in the relatively inactive time periods of soybean meal from 1963 through 1969.

SOYBEAN MEAL #1

	Buy Long May 1	Liquidate July 1	Liquidate Aug 15	Net Profit
1963	61.75	71.00		925
1964	62.00	62.35	63.70	170
1965	62.40	63.40		100
1966	68.20	78.50		1030
1967	70.80	72.00		120
1968	73.75	74.00	74.15	40
1969	68.65	69.50		85
1970	69.75	80.25		1050
1971	76.60	82.30		570
1972	88.75	98.00		925
1973	144.00	195.00		5100
1974	133.00	136.30		330
1975	135.50	130.00	146.30	1080
1976	148.40	215.70		6730

100% CORRECT IN 14 YEARS
18,255 POINTS PROFIT
0 POINTS LOSS
$18,255 PROFIT

Rules:
1. Buy long one contract of March Meal on May 1.
2. Use a 10% stop.
3. Take profits on July 1.
4. If by July 1 the position is at a loss or even, place a 5% stop below entry price. Liquidate the position on August 15.

SOYBEAN MEAL TRADE #2

It's interesting to note here that there is a strong seasonal tendency for prices to rally during the early spring months of the year. However, it is difficult to say exactly when this rally will take place and from what levels. Nonetheless, by using that key point, the April high, we have been able to establish relatively good times when one should get into the market.

Notice, however, that in 1974 and 1975, the usual tendency for the rally to start going places in May or June did not occur until July. Even so, given the trade rules we have developed, one still would have his theoretical profits.

Trades Rules:

Note the high for the March soybean meal in the month of April. If anytime after May 1 that price is penetrated, buy long. The target should be five percent of your entry point, where you automatically take profits.

SOYBEAN MEAL #2

	April High	High Penetrated After May 1	Liquidated At Target	Date Liquidated	Points Profit
1964	62.00	May 3	65.10	July 1	310
1965	64.50	Aug 15	67.72	Sept 11	322
1966	63.20	June 7	66.36	Jan 6	316
1967	68.90	May 23	72.45	June 16	355
1968	72.15	May 23	75.75	Jan 18	360
1969	69.40	May 16	72.87	Oct 15	347
1970	70.75	June 1	74.28	June 22	353
1971	76.25	May 3	80.05	May 25	380
1972	90.60	May 16	95.13	June 26	453
1973	143.00	May 1	150.15	May 9	715
1974	144.80	July 8	152.04	July 15	724
1975	149.00	July 25	156.45	Aug 15	745
1976	148.50	May 4	155.92	May 11	742

100 % CORRECT IN 13 YEARS
6,122 POINTS PROFIT
$6,122 NET PROFIT

Rules:
1. Note April high.
2. Buy when April high is penetrated after May 1.
3. Set a target of 5% of entry price.
4. Liquidate at target.

SOYBEAN OIL

Soybean oil is a by-product of soybeans and has many commercial uses. The price of soybean oil, of course, inter-relates with the price of soybeans and soybean meal vs. competitive oils.

SOYBEAN OIL TRADE #1

The trade has been 70% correct during the last 17 years. It has a net profit of 38.64 cents, a net loss of 2.26 cents and a net gain of 36.38 cents, for a dollar profit of $21,828.

The tabulation on this trade shows an extremely reliable tendency for prices to advance in the December oil contract during the months of June, July and August. The most interesting aspect of this trade is that the risk-reward ratio is way in our favor where we have profits more than ten times losses.

We have a long history to follow, but we should note that the prices for 1960, 1961 and 1962 are again "eyeballed" off of charts, not from our computer printout sheets. In any event, the trade shows a strong seasonal tendency for traders to follow.

Trade Rules:

The trade rules are to buy long December oil on June 19. Use a straight stop of five percent and take profits on August 15.

131

SOYBEAN OIL TRADE #1

	Buy Long June 19	5% Date	Stop Price	Liquidate Aug 15	Profit/ Loss
1960	8.10			8.75	+ 65
1961	10.40			10.80	+ 40
1962	8.75	July 15	8.32		-43
1963	9.37	July 30	8.91		-46
1964	8.31			8.73	+42
1965	8.50			8.83	+33
1966	10.65			12.71	+206
1967	9.77	June 30	9.29		-48
1968	7.67	July 29	7.29		-38
1969	7.16			7.44	+28
1970	10.27	July 6	9.76		-51
1971	12.22			12.77	+55
1972	10.05			10.10	+5
1973	14.90			23.55	+865
1974	25.22			37.55	+1233
1975	15.53			26.15	−1062
1976	18.37			20.67	+230

70% CORRECT
3,864 POINTS PROFIT
226 POINTS LOSS
$21,828 NET PROFIT

Rules:
1. Buy long December Oil on June 19.
2. Use a 5% straight stop.
3. Take profits on August 15.

WHEAT

Although wheat is grown and harvested throughout the world, the United States is one of the largest wheat producing countries. Within the United States, Kansas is the largest producer of wheat. It should be noted that China is also developing rapidly as a wheat growing country, especially in their northeast sector.

The most important statistical information for wheat traders would be the Planting Intentions published by the U. S. Government or the Wheat Situations Report which is published in March, May, August and November of each year.

The United States has two wheat crops--one is referred to as winter wheat which is harvested in the early summer of each year and is responsible for 75% of the total U.S. production. The other is spring wheat which is harvested during the late summer. All of the harvests usually end during the July-August time period.

If you study the seasonal tendency chart, you will notice that wheat has a strong tendency to decline into the year's low in the summer months and then rally. However, trading wheat is not quite that simple. In fact, it was extremely difficult indentifying good wheat seasonal trades in the market.

One of the old standby trades that spread traders will want to pay attention to will be to buy long December wheat, selling short December corn on June 1 and liquidating the spread on November 1. This trade has been correct 68% of the time since 1949. However, there have been some sizable losses when the trade was wrong.

Another old standby would be to spread being short December wheat and long December corn opening the position on March 1 and liquidating on June 1. That trade has produced profits 75% of the time since 1949.

Wheat production in the United States normally exceeds the domestic usage The remaining portion of our wheat production is shipped overseas under the control of the Department of Agriculture for use in everything from foreign negotiations to improving our balance of payments.

Wheat is traded on two major exchanges in the U.S., The Chicago Board of Trade and Kansas City. There is also a Minneapolis Contract of Wheat; however, the one most traders trade is The Chicago Contract. Wheat is broken down into three classifications: soft wheat, hard wheat and durum. Soft wheat is used for cake flour and pastry; hard wheat is used for bread; and durum, the hardest of the wheats, is used for spaghetti and noodles.

We have been able to isolate four good wheat seasonal tendency trades.

WHEAT TRADE #1

This trade has been 86% correct since 1963, with a net profit of 110.5 points, a net loss of 9.3 points and a net gain of $5,050. This trade attempts to take advantage of the fact that wheat rallies late in the fall, and there is an attempted piggyback in the rally which usually starts early in the summer.

Trade Rules:

Buy long one contract March wheat, the second trading day in October. Rule two, take an automatic 20 percent profit. Rule three, use a straight five cent stop. Rule four, close-out with profits; if you have not closed-out the position, do so on November 1. It is interesting to note that the trade has only been wrong two times since 1963 and both of those were for a small loss—in 1975 for 5 cents and in 1967 for 4.3 cents. In recent years, as the markets have increased their volatility, this trade has become more profitable.

WHEAT TRADE #1

	2nd Trading Day in October	5-pt. Stop		20-pt. Target		Liquidate Nov 1	Profit/ Loss
		Date	Price	Date	Price		
1963	208.1					217.1	+9.0
1964	152.3					154.6	+2.3
1965	165.1					168.0	+2.9
1966	174.0					178.5	+4.5
1967	160.1					155.8	-4.3
1968	126.8					134.2	+7.4
1969	138.1					138.7	+.6

	2nd Trading Day in October	5-pt. Stop		20-pt. Target		Liquidate Nov 1	Profit/ Loss
		Date	Price	Date	Price		
1970	170.2					178.0	+7.8
1971	147.7					156.0	+8.3
1972	213.5					221.2	+7.7
1973	451.0			Oct 4	471.0		+20.0
1974	509.2			Oct 4	529.2		+20.0
1975	424.5	Oct 13	419.5				-5.0
1976	301.0			Oct 13	321.0		+20.0

86% CORRECT SINCE 1963
110.5 POINTS PROFIT
9.3 POINTS LOSS
$5,050 NET PROFIT

Rules:
1. Buy long March wheat on the second trading day in October.
2. Use a straight stop of 5¢.
3. Take a 20¢ profit.
4. If 20¢ profit has not been taken, liquidate position on November 1.

WHEAT TRADE #2

Since 1960 this trade has been correct 70% of the time, with net profits of 260.7 cents, net losses of 35.5 cents, for a total net gain of 225.2 cents or $11,260. During the last 17 years the trade has been incorrect on five separate occasions.

This trade attempts to take advantage of the fact that wheat declines, usually, in the spring of the year into the summer lows most often seen in the July-August time period.

Trade Rules:

The trade rules are simple. Sell short one contract of December wheat on February 27. If February 27 is not a Friday, wait until the next Friday and sell short. Liquidate the short position on April 1.

	Sell Short	Liquidate April 1	Profit/ Loss
1960	191.0	190.0	+1.0
1961	206.0	196.5	+9.5
1962	216.0	217.0	-1.0
1963	199.5	194.0	+5.5
1964	169.0	165.0	+4.0
1965	152.0	149.0	+3.0
1966	162.0	161.5	+ .5
1967	182.5	188.0	-5.5
1968	158.0	159.0	-1.0
1969	139.5	135.5	+4.0
1970	144.0	139.0	+5.0
1971	160.0	157.5	+2.5
1972	159.0	158.0	+1.0
1973	223.0	216.3	+6.7
1974	570.0	400.0	+170.0
1975	357.0	385.0	-28.0
1976	424.0	376.0	+48.0

70% CORRECT SINCE 1960
260.7 POINTS PROFIT
35.5 POINTS LOSS
$11,260 NET PROFIT

Rules:
1. Sell short December wheat on February 27. If February 27 is not a Friday, wait for the next trading Friday to sell short.
2. Liquidate the position on April 1.

WHEAT TRADE #3

This is perhaps one of the most impressive seasonal tendency trades we have isolated. Not necessarily because of the dollar amounts or the percentage correctness, but because we were able to go back in this particular case to 1957 with wheat prices. Thus, we have a total time period of 20 years to study the tendency of this trade. During that time period, it has produced net profits of 400.9 cents, net losses of 31.9 cents, net gain of 369.0 cents or a profit of $18,450. It has been correct 80% of the time. In other words, 16 times out of 20. Obviously, we are inclined to believe a great deal in seasonal tendencies, and certainly think data such as this covering a time span of 20 years is most impressive evidence to support our position.

Trade Rules:

Trade rules are very basic: you sell short one contract of December wheat on March 15; if prices are higher on May 1 by 1.5 cents, reverse, going long. If you are short, liquidate the short position on June 1. If you reversed to the long side, liquidate the long position on August 1. The trade has scored some excellent gains; perhaps, however, one should kick out the gains scored in 1973 of 133.7 points—but even that year fit with the overall seasonal tendency. The tendency, of course, is for prices to decline during the March-April-May-June time period. In the event that we have not seen a decline, it is suggestive of an earlier than normal bull move which begins late in the summer. If one had followed that advice, he would have reversed correctly for the bull moves that began in 1966, 1970 and 1973. The only exception was 1962, when the reversal signal was wrong and the year showed a net loss.

Notice the losses for this trade are very small, especially compared to the profits.

WHEAT TRADE #3

	Sell Short March 15	Price May 1	Loss Loss on Reversal	Liquidation June 1	Liquidation August 1	Profit/ Loss
1957	225.1	213.7		209.2		+159
1958	200.8	194.7		192.7		+81
1959	194.5	195.2		192.2		+23
1960	191.8	192.6		193.0		-12
1961	199.1	197.7		196.0		+31
1962	216.3	221.0	-4.7		217.8	-32
1963	195.1	194.0		192.0		+31
1964	164.0	158.0		157.5		+65
1965	150.5	146.6		146.5		+40
1966	162.2	166.2	-4.0		193.3	+271
1967	190.7	177.8		176.3		+144
1968	164.1	146.7		145.7		+184
1969	137.7	137.7		136.3		+13

	Sell Short March 15	Price May 1	Loss Loss on Reversal	Liquidation June 1	Liquidation August 1	Profit/ Loss
1970	144.0	148.2	-4.2		152.3	+41
1971	161.2	156.5		161.3		-1
1972	155.2	152.2		151.3		+39
1973	211.5	226.0	-14.5		359.7	+1337
1974	468.0	375.0		375.0		+930
1975	366.0	332.0		318.0		+480
1976	390.0	354.0		376.0		+140

85% CORRECT IN 20 YEARS
4009 POINTS PROFIT
319 POINTS LOSS
$18,450 NET PROFIT

Rules:
1. Sell short December Wheat on March 15.
2. If prices are higher on May 1 by 1½¢, reverse position and go long.
3. Liquidate short position on June 1.
4. Liquidate long position on August 1.

WHEAT TRADE #4

This trade has produced a loss only one time during the past 14 years, which means its profitability is 93% with a gain of 434.0 points, a loss of 39.4 points and a total gain of 394.6 cents of $19,730.

This trade is based on wheat prices reaching important bottoms and strong rallies in the latter half of each year.

Trade Rules:

The rules for this trade are very basic. Purchase long one contract of March wheat on June 15. Use a reverse stop of 2% of the closing price on June 15. If you reverse to the short side on the 2% reversal stop figure, reverse back to a long side if prices close above the original entry price on June 15. Liquidate position, longs or shorts, on August 10.

This trade has had substantial profits, but, of course, they come in the 1973 through

1976 time period when the wheat market was more volatile. Nonetheless, there were some sizable profits in the 1960's----especially considering the volatility of the market at those points. It's noteworthy that the greatest loss in the trade was 10.8 points, which occurred in 1973, when one was reversed to the short side and reversed back to the long side before the bull move began. The only time the trade was not profitable was in 1963 when there was a loss of 5.3 points on the first long position and, when one reversed, he netted out 3.9 points for a loss for the year of 1.4 points, which was the only losing year in the sample studied. This, of course, is a very small loss compared to the average gains, showing one more example of seasonal reliability.

WHEAT TRADE #4

	Buy Long June 15	REVERSE TO SHORT 2% STOP			REVERSE TO LONG 2% STOP			Liquidate Aug 10	Profit/ Loss
		Date	Price	Loss	Date	Price	Loss		
1963	197.5	July 11	192.2	-5.3				188.3	+3.9
1964	156.3	June 25	153.2	-3.1				149.0	+4.2
1965	149.1							157.0	+7.9
1966	186.0							198.0	+12.0
1967	170.7	June 27	167.3	-3.4				161.5	+5.8
1968	144.2	July 1	141.4	-2.8				132.7	+8.7
1969	140.0	July 16	137.2	-2.8				133.6	+3.6
1970	149.3							153.2	+3.9
1971	170.2	June 22	168.1	-3.4				148.2	+19.9
1972	150.6							¹87.5	+36.9
1973	273.0	June 21	267.6	-5.4	July 2	273.0	-5.4	431.2	+158.2
1974	406.5							453.5	+47.0
1975	321.5							412.5	+91.0
1976	391.5	July 19	383.7	-7.8				352.7	+31.0

93% CORRECT IN 14 YEARS
4340 POINTS GAIN
394 POINTS LOSS
$19,730 NET GAIN

Rules:

1. Buy long March Wheat on June 15.
2. Use a 2% stop, reversing position to the short side if stop is hit.
3. If position is reversed to the shortside, reverse back to a long position if prices close above the original entry price on June 15.
4. Liquidate position on August 10.

SEASONAL TENDENCY OF

COMMODITY MARKET SPREADS

Data for the following chapter has been excerpted in parts from a seasonal spread booklet written by Robert D. Robens, Commodity Research Director, Hornblower Weeks Hemphill, & Noyes. There are several extremely profitable seasonal spread trades that we want to mention in this chapter. We will begin by listing the seasonal spreads that Mr. Robens has discovered and will then close the chapter with the seasonal spreads we have found to be workable.

In writing about his seasonal spread trades, Mr. Robens has said, *"Seasonal price movements are a function of 'normal' conditions and relationships that economists and analysts often rely upon for recommendations and projections. For seasonals to be reliable it is important to identify the significant variables that are the primary motivating forces for change. In commodities, these variables often center around crop production and harvest considerations, free stocks and inventories, domestic consumption and export demand.*

Spreads are simply price relationships which exist in change between commodity futures contract months or between different commodities. These price relationships often have characteristic behavorial patterns resulting from certain repeated fundamental considerations. This study has presented a few of the most reliable seasonal spreads and identified some of the primary motivating forces indigenous to that reliablity."

In his work Mr. Robens sought to find spread trades that had a reliability factor between 60 and 70%. Unfortunately, he did not compile a list of the profits that one would have achieved following his spread trade suggestions; nonetheless, spread traders should find his study fascinating.

We will list the various commodities one at a time, and then give the spread trades for that particular commodity.

141

CORN

The first seasonal spread trade for corn is to buy long July, sell short May during January, liquidating the spread in April. Also, in the month of January and sometimes in February it would have been profitable to buy long December, selling short May, liquidating that spread trade in March or April. During the month of February and March Mr. Roben's works suggest that it would be profitable to buy long May, selling short September, liquidating that spread trade during the month of May. It also appears that it would be profitable to buy long May, sell short December, during March-April, liquidating during the month of May. Also during the March and April time period, buying long July versus short September, liquidating during the month of June. There is also a seasonal trade to buy long May, sell short July, during the first part of May, liquidating it during the month of May. In October there is a seasonal trade to buy long December, sell short March, liquidate in December. In October and November the trade is to buy long September corn, selling short May corn, liquidating the trade the following February and March.

CHICAGO WHEAT

The seasonal tendency here would be to buy the March contract, selling short the May, during the July-August time period, liquidating the spread in December. Also, buy long December, sell short September during the April-May time period, liquidating in August; and finally buying long December and selling short March during the August-September time frame, liquidating in December.

CATTLE

In the cattle complex there is another very reliable spread trade one can put on during the next to last week in January each year. The trade is to be long April cattle, short August cattle. The trade works simply because of that strong seasonal tendency for nearby cattle prices to rally during the first part of the year. The spread trader taking advantage of this seasonal tendency should take an automatic 100 point profit and use a 50 point straight stop on the trade. Had one done this starting in 1965 he would have taken 100 points in 1965 and 1966, 75 points in 1967, 100 points in 1968, 100 points in 1969, 100 points in 1970, 100 points in 1971, broken even in 1972, 100 points in 1973 and had a loss in 1974 of 50 points. As you can see, the results of this tendency are high profits (8.50 or $3,400) and one which cattle traders will want to watch closely.

A strong seasonal tendency for the cattle spread traders to take note would be that of long December, short June and expecting the spread to decline starting in September of each year. This has occurred in 1965, 1966, 1969, 1970, 1972, 1973, and 1974.

COPPER

Those of you who follow the copper market should follow a spread trade being long July, short December expecting an increase in the nearby months.

The trade rules are that one should put the spread on the first week in January each year, taking an automatic 300 point profit. The trade developed 300 points profit in 1965, 66, 68, 69, 73 & 74. The variable years are 1972, with a loss of approximately 50 points, 1974 with a gain of approximately 150 points; in 1970 there was a loss of 250 points and in 1967 there was a loss of 250 points. It seems advisable for the spread trader to *limit* losses on this spread trade to 100 points, should the spread move that much against you, once the spread is placed. The spread obviously takes advantage of the fact that copper prices tend to rally during the first part of every year. Net gain here was 1,400 points of $3,500.

COTTON

There is one apparent seasonal tendency in cotton for spread traders. The trade calls for one to be long March, short December placing the spread on the last week in November each year, expecting a profit of 200 points. The 200-point profit was taken in 1965, 1966, 1967, 1969, 1970 and 1971. There were losing trades in 1972 and then profitable trades again in 1973, 1974, 1975 and 1976. We would suggest placing a stop of 100 points on the trade, in the event that the seasonal tendency does not become operative.

EGGS

This trade suggests the trader should be short May, long September, placing the trade on March 1. The trade should be kept on until the May contract expires. Had this been done, one would have obtained profits in 1969 of 600 points, in 1970 of 100 points, in 1971 of 180 points, in 1972 of 250 points, in 1973 of 350 points, in 1974 of 750 points and 1975 for 400 points.

This is an interesting trade in that it has been correct 100% of the time, and for substantial amounts of money. Obviously, traders should follow it closely.

Buy long July, sell short March and September liquidating the trade the following march. Continuing the trade, buy long July; sell short August during the April-May time period (liquidating July-August in July). Also sell short July during October-November, liquidating March-April. Finally, buy long January, sell short July during the March-April time period, liquidating during July.

SOYBEANS

Buy long July, liquidate during March and September liquidating the trade the following March. Continuing the trades, buy long July sell short August during the April-May time period (liquidating July-August in July); also buy long August sell short July during October-November, liquidating March-April, and finally, buy long January sell short July during the March-April time period, liquidating during July.

SOYBEAN OIL

Buy long October, sell short September during February and March, liquidating during July. Buy long August, sell short December during the June-July time period, liquidating in August.

OATS

Buy long July sell short May and January, liquidating in April.

SEASONAL SPREAD TRADES
WE HAVE BEEN ABLE TO ISOLATE IN THE MARKET

The Heart Attack Spread

A few years ago a broker devised what he called the "breakfast spread"--long bellies (bacon) and short eggs. Unfortunately, the spread did not work and the chap not only lost all his money, clients, wife and house, but had a heart attack in the process. As he awoke in the hospital's emergency room, he asked the gentlemen lying in beds on both side of him what triggered their heart attacks.

You guessed it——one patient's malady was caused by commodities, the other by stocks!

The spread trades and seasonal trades presented here are not of the heart attack variety. They have all been thoroughly researched. For your convenience, they are given in chronological order.

144

We have been able to find only two pork belly spreads that work well. Both spreads given here have been correct all the time--100% accurate. This is due to interactions of the market place and seasonal tendencies. These tendencies are so powerful that we suspect the trades will always work as well in the future as they have in the past.

PORK BELLY SPREAD #1

March vs May--Yin and Yang in the Belly Market

This trading opportunity has not presented itself very often--only five times in the last eleven years, so don't hold your breath waiting for it. However, if the conditions arise, take advantage of the trade. This trade is based on the fact that carrying charges in the belly market are about 65% per month. Thus normally March will sell for about $1.30 more than May at the maximum point of weakness. Should March sell for anything less than that, there would be a tremendous imbalance in the marketplace that commercial forces would utilize, and do utilize, to make money.

Trade Rules:

1.   Anytime March bellies sell for 100 points under May go long March, short May. However, do not initiate the trade after January 15 of the year when there are only two months of trading left.

2.   Any time you have a 200 point profit, take it.

3.   Should the spread go from –100 to –10 or higher and then fall back to unity or zero (March and May selling at the same price) close out the trade.

4.   If rules two and three have not gone into operation, close out the trade the last week the March contract trades.

In late February, 1967, the spread dipped below –100 for one week, then shot like a rocket to +130, netting us our automatic 200 point profit.

In 1969 during the middle of June, the spread again fell to –100 during the week. From this point, the spread also moved to +130 again giving us a 200 point "cinch" profit.

In December 1970 the spread went to March under May and stayed there for four months but finally took off closing out at zero for a gain of 100 points.

In 1973 we had a wild market when we again saw prices dip to our overextended yin or weakness state at –100 and then rally above +10 only to fall back to zero, where we took a 100 point profit.

In 1974 the price spread fell to –100, then went a little lower and stayed there four months before taking off, with March going 800 points over May. We would have taken our automatic profit of 200 points.

All in all we then had five trades with a gross profit of $2,880 before commissions. No losses were incurred and we had an average gain of $550. The trade works simply because we get too much weakness, yin, in the spread relationship and commercial forces will right this wrong.

A SEASONAL "SURE THING" SPREAD IN BELLIES

If this book does nothing else, we hope it makes the point that commodity trading need not be the risk laden undertaking bankers and stock brokers make it out to be. It can be "sure thing trading" when one uses a professional approach to selecting and timing his trades.

The next spread you should know about is another one of those rare 100% correct trades. Frankly, this spread alone is well worth the price of this book. You see, market information is worth absolutely nothing or worth much more than you could ever hope to pay for it. This spread falls into the latter category.

PORK BELLY SPREAD #2

One Spread---Two Profits

The spread is to be long the distant February future and short the nearby July future. In other words, be long February 1978 and short July 1977 during the calendar year of 1977.

The trade works due to consumer demand and commercial output. It takes no genius to realize that the consumption of bacon declines during the hotter summer months. That's why the July contract has a pronounced tendency to be weaker than the February contract during May and June.

This spread is unique in that it presents two opportunities to put on the spread--one starting May 1 and then again when the May bellies go off the board about May 21 of each year.

146

Trade Rules:

1. Put the spread on the first trading day in May at the previous day's closing price of the spread. If it is not filled during the day, then instruct your broker to do the spread on the close

2. Tell your broker to take an automatic profit of 200 points any time the spread widens that much in your favor. (When bellies were less volatile than current prices, the order would have been to take an automatic 100 point profit.)

3. If you are unable to close out profitably by June 1, close out on the market date closest to the calendar date of June 15.

Double Header Rules

The same spread can be put on one day after the May option expires. In this case, again, liquidate for an automatic profit of 200 points. If you have not ben able to take the profit by June 15, close out the trade on the market day closest to June 15.

The spread is shown in a chart so you can see how it works. You can see the double top effect allowing you to place the spread on at two different times.

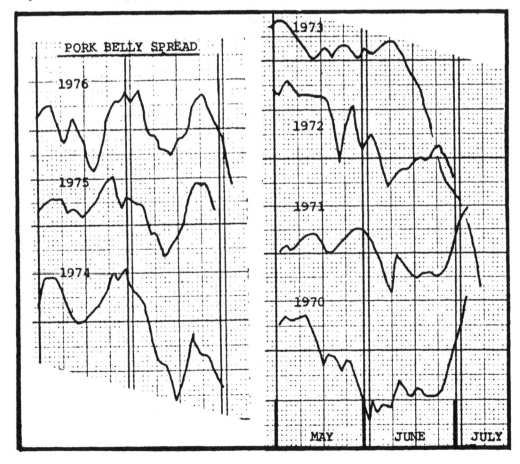

The results are as follows for putting the spread on May 1:

Year	Pt. Profit	$ Profit
1966	+100	$360
1967	+100	$360
1968	+200	$360
1968	+200	$720
1969	+150	$540
1970	+200	$720
1971	+100	$360
1972	+200	$720
1973	+200	$720
1974	+200	$720
1975	+200	$720
1976	+200	$720

The historical record of the trade being put on May 21 is as follows:

Year	Pt. Profit	$ Profit
1970	+200	$720
1971	+200	$720
1972	+200	$720
1973	+200	$720
1974	+200	$720
1975	+200	$720

Unfortunately we have not been able to find any other belly spread trades. But the above ones have a strong historical precedent of making money and must both clearly rate among the very best trades one can find in his pursuit of ideal commodity trades.

Chronological Index

DATE	COMMODITY	TRADE NUMBER
January		
January 1	August Bellies	Trade #1
January 1	May Beans	Trade #1
January 1	April Cattle	Trade #1
January 4	November Beans	Trade #2
January 15	May Oats	Trade #4
January 18	December Corn	Trade #1
January 19	September Copper	Trade #2
February		
February 1	December Copper	Trade #1
February 27	December Wheat	Trade #2
March		
March 1	August Cattle	Trade #3
March 1	August Hogs	Trade #2
March 1	November Beans	Trade #5
March 15	December Wheat	Trade #3
April		
April 1	August Cattle	Trade #2
April 1	September Copper	Trade #4
April 1	September Eggs	Trade #1
April 1	August Hogs	Trade #2
April 1	July Beans	Trade #3
April 12	July Bellies	Trade #2
April 18	August Bellies	Trade #6

DATE	COMMODITY	TRADE NUMBER
May		
May 1	January Copper	Trade #3
May 1	December Flax	Trade #1
May 1	March Meal	Trade #1
May 1	March Meal	Trade #2
May 6	July Oats	Trade #2
May 15	December Corn	Trade #4
May 15	November Beans	Trade #8
June		
June 1	December Cotton	Trade #1
June 15	March Wheat	Trade #4
June 19	December Oil	Trade #1
June 26	November Beans	Trade #6
July		
July 1	August Hogs	Trade #4
July 1	December Oats	Trade #3
July 1	February Bellies	Trade #5
August		
August 3	September Eggs	Trade #2
August 10	February Bellies	Trade #3
August 10	November Beans	Trade #7
August 15	April Cattle	Trade #4
August 20	October Hogs	Trade #3
September		
September 1	December Corn	Trade #3
September 15	November Eggs	Trade #3
September 30	November Beans	Trade #4
October		
October 1	May Potatoes	Trade #1
October 2	March Wheat	Trade #1
October 14	December Corn	Trade #2
November		
November 1	April Hogs	Trade #1
November 1	July Bellies	Trade #4
December		
December 1	May Plywood	Trade #1
December 1	December Oats	Trade #1
December 15	August Cattle	Trade #5
December 15	March Orange Juice	Trade #1